Teaching with Adolescent Learning in Mind

Glenda Ward Beamon

foreword by
Robert J. Marzano

Arlington Heights, Illinois

Teaching With Adolescent Learning in Mind

Published by SkyLight Professional Development
2626 S. Clearbrook Dr., Arlington Heights, IL 60005
800-348-4474 or 847-290-6600
Fax 847-290-6609
info@skylightedu.com
http://www.skylightedu.com

Director, Product Development: Carol Luitjens
Senior Acquisitions Editor: Jean Ward
Editor: Peggy Kulling
Project Coordinator: Donna Ramirez
Cover Designer and Illustrator: David Stockman
Book Designer: Bruce Leckie
Production Supervisor: Bob Crump

LCCCN 00-108402
ISBN 1-57517-329-8

2746V
Item Number 2092
Z Y X W V U T S R Q P O N M L K J I H G F E D C B A
08 07 06 05 04 03 02   15 14 13 12 11 10 9 8 7 6 5 4 3 2

There are
one-story intellects,
two-story intellects, and
three-story intellects with skylights.

All fact collectors, who have no aim beyond their facts, are

one-story minds.

Two-story minds
compare, reason, generalize,
using the labors of the fact collectors
as well as their own.

Three-story minds
idealize, imagine, predict—their best illumination
comes from above,

through the **skylight.**

—Oliver Wendell Holmes

Dedication

To Dave, my mentor and friend, and
the keeper of my dreams.
And to Larry who holds my heart.

Acknowledgments

Writing this book has given me a better understanding of distributed intelligence, for the final product reflects the thoughts of many. To each, I offer sincere appreciation.

To Heather, John, and Holly who invited me into their classrooms, and to Deborah, Nancy, and Teresa who shared their experiences. I commend their enthusiasm for adolescent learning.

To Nathan, Kate, and the other adolescents who shared their dreams and insight. Their candor validates what we believe is true about the learning needs of today's youth.

To my students, August, Clair, Elizabeth, Kathy, Mechelle, Sherra, and Suzanne, for sharing their ideas as prospective middle school teachers. They should do well.

To my friend Dayna for her careful appraisal and collegial support. Her spirit and commitment to adolescents is celebrated in these pages.

To Michael and Brent, Kenneth and Beth, our adult sons and daughter, for their interest and resourcefulness. Their experiences, good and sad, helped to shape this story.

To my parents, Claude and Polly Ward, for their support of my endeavor, once again. Their unwavering pride makes me believe that anything is possible.

And most importantly, to Larry, my husband, for his patience, understanding, and valued assistance. He enhanced my ideas with astute and realistic perspective, and he gave depth to my vision.

Contents

Foreword

The next decade will surely see some significant changes in K–12 education. One of those changes will be increased access to the research and theory on human learning and the utilization of that research and theory in classrooms. That body of literature will inform us about those instructional techniques that work best with specific types of students in specific contexts, breaking the current paradigm of "one type of schooling fits all."

Glenda Beamon's book, *Teaching with Adolescent Learning in Mind,* is a giant step in that direction, particularly with regard to adolescents. With an impressive command of the extant research and theory, Beamon not only informs us of the cognitive, metacognitive, and affective forces at work in the daily lives of adolescents, but she spells out how to utilize those forces to enhance learning.

This book is a potentially powerful resource for classroom teachers as well as building and district-level administrators. In the hands of thoughtful educators, *Teaching with Adolescent Learning in Mind* can go a long way to improving education for adolescents from all backgrounds.

ROBERT J. MARZANO
Senior Fellow
Mid-continent Research for
Education and Learning

Preface

Teaching adolescents involves energy, patience, resourcefulness, and a good sense of humor. They would rather talk about the latest movie than discuss Shakespearean tragedy. They put more thought into what to do Friday night than a lab experiment. They worry about looking "right," being liked, and being included. They fear failure, making the wrong choices, change, death, and the future. Boisterously, yet precariously negotiating the middle ground of youth, adolescents have the cognitive capacity to learn to regulate their own thinking and learning, but often lack the emotional judgment to assess its quality. Their motivation to learn may vary from subject to subject, class to class, teacher to teacher, day to day, even hour to hour. They differ in experience, knowledge, interest, ability, social status, and emotional need, and they fill our classrooms to capacity.

Some things have not changed about adolescents since I began teaching them over twenty-five years ago. The awkward, tentative, and glorious ritual of youth is still about negotiating relationships and shaping identity. Intellectually, these students are capable of assuming increasing responsibility for their decisions and actions, yet they need continued support and guidance to develop the skills and confidence. The context for adolescence, however, has changed dramatically. Growing up in an era of instantaneous and boundless access, today's adolescents bring a different set of experiences and needs to the classroom. They also face a future where the capacity to manage vast quantities of information and to communicate effectively are necessary skills. These changes have significant implications for what happens in today's classrooms.

Many teachers have responded to the challenge of preparing a new generation of adolescents for college and the work place, and this book is written in their celebration. Recognizing their students' need for pertinence, these teachers center instruction on relevant issues and reality-based problems. Noting adolescents' need to question and explore, they incorporate student-directed inquiry, interpretation, debate, and analysis. Understanding their need for active and social

*Your
Ideas*

involvement, they allow for collaboration, and realizing their propensity for technology, they provide opportunities for electronic access and connection. Also, in recognition of adolescents' need for stronger content in a knowledge-driven society, they teach more conceptually. These teachers create learning experiences that respond to the social, emotional, and cognitive needs of today's adolescents, and their efforts prepare them well for the future that awaits us all.

This book also acknowledges the challenging circumstances in middle and high school classrooms. The pressures and expectations on teachers far exceed the time and energy of the most conscientious. The push for coverage and the direct assessment of information tend to restrain instruction to a mode that maximizes teacher delivery and minimizes student interaction. Time is limited, students are many and varied, and the responsibilities are immense. Unfortunately, in this existing culture, adolescents' social, personal, and intellectual needs are often unmet, and their understanding of content and the critical strategies for learning management are limited.

The observations, interviews, and experiences that inspired this book, nevertheless, uncovered a more promising story. Regardless of external demands and daily challenges, many teachers are undaunted in their efforts to create learning environments that remain responsive to the needs of adolescents. These teachers have "made it work," and their generosity is reflected in the pages that follow. These are the teachers that students talk about, and their classes are the ones they describe.

Introduction

Teaching adolescents effectively requires an understanding of who they are, how they think, learn and feel, and of the impact of curricular and instructional decisions on the quality of their learning experiences. The goal of this book is to help to create this understanding. It is written for preservice and practicing teachers of adolescents, and for teacher educators. Its intent is to profile the adolescent as a learner whose intellectual, emotional, and social needs must be considered primary in the learning process. *Teaching with Adolescent Learning in Mind's* ultimate purpose is to affirm the strategic and powerful role of the teacher in structuring a responsive, supportive, and challenging learning environment for adolescents.

Teaching adolescents is more challenging than in past decades. Raised in an era of easy access and early exposure, these youth know more questions to ask and how to find answers more quickly. They are impatient with redundancy and skeptical until proof is apparent. They are irritated when their teachers do not have control, do not know their subjects, or try too hard to be "cool." Unfortunately, many adolescents are enticed by experiences far more appealing than those found in the typical classroom, and they often see little relevance to what they are learning there. What is equally disturbing is that many students are graduating from high school with limited understanding of content and with minimal practice in the cognitive skills necessary to attain this understanding (Gardner 1999, Wiggins and McTigue 1998).

So much is acknowledged about the classroom conditions and instructional practices that best promote adolescent thinking and learning, yet the observed variability in methodology, level of student involvement, nature of assessment, and physical environment suggests vastly differing perceptions among teachers. In the new millennium, the specialization of knowledge will be imperative, global competition will be the norm, and "thinking for a living" will be the expectation (Marsh 1999). Adolescents will also need the skills for emotional control, reasoned decision making, and moral judgment. They must be prepared

ACT
Adolescent
Centered
Teaching

for their future, and for a certain quality of life. This book addresses this important challenge.

Teaching with Adolescent Learning in Mind introduces early, and develops with ongoing applications, pertinent concepts related to adolescent learning, including metacognition, motivation, social cognition, and self-regulation. The content examples and scenarios are based primarily on observations and interviews with practitioners and adolescents. Underlying each are the elements of relevance, active learning, content depth, collaboration, inquiry, challenge, student ownership, ongoing assessment, and guided reflection. Consistently important throughout is the role of the teacher in planning for and guiding adolescents' learning, and their social, emotional, and intellectual development.

The intent of *Teaching with Adolescent Learning in Mind* is not to offer packaged lesson plans for easy application. Teaching adolescents is not that simple. An understanding of their social, emotional, and intellectual needs is developed by knowing them as learners and by making critical connections between long-standing and current theory and its implication for instructional practice. The book's purpose is to offer teachers, through discussion and example, a conceptual and flexible framework on which to base daily decisions about content and pedagogy. The Adolescent-Centered Teaching (ACT) Models in each chapter are designed as illustrations of this framework. Each ACT further features specific concepts developed within each chapter.

The format for each ACT encapsulates the following research-based instructional components, each of which promotes adolescent learning and metacognitive development.

- Content understanding, which involves an emphasis on the essential understandings of the discipline and pertinent state and national curricular standards;
- Strategies for inquiry, which focus on adolescent motivation and challenge through intriguing and authentic events, problems and questions;
- Guided interaction, which promotes the teacher's role as active facilitator as students set up strategies for inquiry, proceed through the learning experiences, and become progressively self-directive; and
- Metacognitve development and assessement, during which adolescents are involved in evaluation, reflection, and the transfer of learning to comparable and extended experiences.

Chapter 1 profiles the adolescent as learner and thinker. Adolescent intellectual, social, and emotional development is described with focus on the emerging capacity for metacognition and self-regulated learning. Adolescent motivation is discussed in terms of personal beliefs about competence and of perceptions of relevance in learning experiences. Their learning is enhanced by intellectually challenging content and tasks, personal choice, responsibility, and meaningful inter-action with others in the instructional context.

Chapter 2 portrays today's adolescents as a generation that has outgrown the practices and boundaries of the traditional classroom. Many graduate without a true understanding of content, unpracticed in the skills of intellectual engagement and problem solving, and with few cognitive strategies for independent learning management. Teaching them effectively calls for a better understanding of how they think, learn, and feel, and of the practices that positively affect their educa-tional experiences and future preparation.

Chapter 3 proposes a learning environment that is responsive to the affective, cognitive, and social needs of the adolescent. An adolescent-centered perspective is described in terms of the important interaction among adolescent learner, learning, and learning environment. Several factors are discussed that affect adolescent learning, including stu-dents' emotions, teacher and student dispositions, learner autonomy, learning context, and interpersonal connection. Multiple examples illus-trate these interacting social, affective, and cognitive dimensions.

Chapter 4 examines current cognitive, social-cognitive, and social-emotional research with emphasis on knowledge construction, mastery of content, thinking development, interpersonal relationships, and social interaction. A central premise is that adolescent learning is an active, emotional, and socially-shared process of higher-order knowledge build-ing for understanding. The teacher is less directive as adolescents assume increasing responsibility for personal learning management. Supporting content examples connect learning theory with practice.

Chapter 5 more explicitly develops teachers' strategic role in structuring an environment for adolescent thinking and learning. Specific instructional strategies that facilitate inquiry, problem solving, content integration, and collaboration are highlighted. These strategies include problem-based learning, Web-based and other technology-enhanced projects and simulations, seminars, and cooperative learning.

Chapter 6 explores instructional practices that are conducive to learning transfer. It further explores adolescent thinking and learning within the subject areas of mathematics, social studies, science, lan-guage arts, and the fine arts. The appendix, Internet Resources, allows

*Your
Ideas*

the readers easy reference to the nearly one hundred Web sites mentioned in the text.

Teaching with Adolescent Learning in Mind addresses the complex interplay between the teacher, the adolescent learner, and the factors in the learning environment in a way that is conceptually and instructionally manageable. The ultimate goal of educators who teach adolescents is that their students will complete secondary education with a strong understanding of content, with the social and emotional skills for productivity and lifetime learning, and with the intrinsic motivation for intellectual pursuit and societal contribution.

1

Understanding the Adolescent as Learner

More Different than Alike

Any attempt to typify adolescents is challenged by a simple look inside a middle or high school classroom. Beneath plaid shirts and loose-fitting tees, under denim and khaki, in tennis shoes and squared-off boots, with caps and without, trend-setting or trend-defying, adolescents are a group of individuals who differ by size, shape, age, race, taste, gender, ethnicity, and socioeconomic status. Their interests, personalities, abilities, needs, and experiences are as varied as their attitudes, beliefs, perceptions, and feelings. What they fear, what they value, what they anticipate, and what they trust differ. The circumstances of their births, the events of their lives, and the expectations of their respective cultures have shaped each in unique ways. They are different in what they know, how they express themselves, and in what they need in order to learn.

The heterogeneous, multicultural, and multilingual adolescent population is increasingly complex. Language, custom, and value systems distinguish students, as does access to opportunity, privilege, and

*Your
Ideas*

*Give an
example*

support. Some are physically and mentally fit, while others require special accommodation to learn and interact effectively in the instructional environment. Some understand advanced calculus, while others struggle daily with Algebra I. Some love to read Arthurian legend, while others prefer a drafting table and a straight edge. Some like country and western music; others choose rock or rap. Some have had positive experiences with school and enjoy learning, while others are playing a waiting game for a time they hope will be better.

Adolescents today are more or less confident, more or less sophisticated, more or less motivated, more or less capable, and more or less prepared. They achieve differently within different content areas, they approach problems in different ways, they exhibit different kinds of intelligence, they indicate different learning preferences, and they need different ways to show their understanding (Gallagher, J. J. and Gallagher, S. A. 1994; Gardner 1993; Renzulli 1998; Sternberg 1985; 1988). Stated another way, students have "different kinds of minds and therefore learn, remember, perform, and understand in different ways" (Gardner 1991, 11).

While teachers have little control over the magnitude of factors that make adolescents uniquely who they are, they do have the power to make strategic decisions that affect their learning. Teachers who teach with adolescent learning in mind do the following:

- ask students about their personal strengths, preferences, and interests, and incorporate these into planning;
- find out what students know or remember, and help them relate to new learning by building connections;
- look for broad themes in the content to include a wider range of students' ideas;
- help students make a bridge between subject matter and real life;
- vary tasks to accommodate individual learning strengths and preferences;
- structure groups that are flexible to validate interests and a range of learning abilities;
- give assignments that differentiate for students' varying learning needs;
- allow students to discuss, explore, wonder, and question;
- listen, guide, encourage, expect, push, facilitate, and challenge;
- celebrate adolescents' individuality by letting their thoughts be heard and their creativity flourish;
- allow students to work, talk and, question together;
- permit students to delve into and better understand content through direct, meaningful, and relevant involvement;

- challenge students to use knowledge in a way that makes sense and a difference in their lives and others;
- trust and guide students to make decisions about their learning;
- respect and value adolescents' differences and help them become more competent and confident in personal learning management; and
- allow students to expand the horizons of learning to tap and interact with resources in the local and global communities.

Your Ideas

Adolescents need to be understood as complex individuals who bring diverse perspectives to the learning context (McCombs and Whisler 1997). Varied and random biological and environmental factors have affected how they feel about themselves and how they view school in general. Though all are capable of learning, none responds uniformly to one style of teaching, one curriculum, one mode of assessment, one cultural perspective, or, necessarily, one language. A sensitivity to their differences lends validation to who they are and what they have to contribute as learners. Teachers who respect differences among adolescents create caring classroom communities that show students they are valued, their ideas are supported, and their feelings are important. Consideration for personal differences, however, is sometimes missing in classrooms. According to adolescents, it is that consideration that matters most (Sizer 1996).

Adolescent Thinking and Learning

Understanding the adolescent as learner ultimately means understanding how and under what conditions learning best occurs (Lambert and McCombs 1998). Learning is believed to be a natural, ongoing, and active process of constructing meaning from information and experience. It is an intuitive and universal human capacity that enables, from an early age, the mastery of symbolic systems such as language, music, and mathematics (Gardner 1991). Learning is an internally mediated process that is controlled primarily by the learner and is affected by his or her motivation, perceptions, skills, and knowledge. Learning is an intellectual process highly influenced by social interaction and situational context, in addition to personal beliefs, dispositions, and emotions (see Figure 1.1).

For adolescent learning to occur, a few things generally happen. First, adolescents are able to connect what they are trying to learn with what they already know, understand, or have personally experienced. Secondly, they are favorably inclined, or motivated, to put forth the necessary effort and time. Adolescent learning, however, is not merely

The Adolescent Perspective

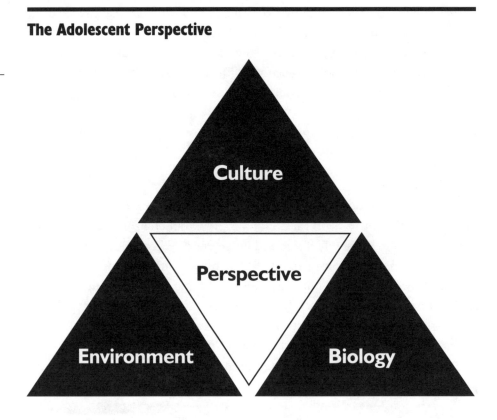

Figure 1.1

about building on prior knowledge, getting students excited about a topic, reassuring them that they are capable of the work, or keeping them on-task (Perkins 1992; Sizer 1996). Adolescent learning involves interactive, purposeful, and meaningful engagement. It happens best under the following circumstances:

- **Adolescents "do something" that makes sense in a larger context, such as confronting real-life issues and problems.** For example, the complexity of citizens' rights is better understood when students follow legislative debates over gun control and discuss continuing problems of school violence.
- **Their personal initiative and energy are moved into action through meaningful involvement with relevant and current content.** For example, health issues take on new meaning when students conduct a research awareness campaign on the life-threatening impact of cigarette smoking and discuss the ethics of juvenile-targeted advertisement.

Your Ideas

- **Their cognitive and affective capabilities are challenged, such as when connections are made between difficult content and its application to personal experiences.** For example, physics gains relevance when adolescents observe the movement of playground equipment at the neighborhood park.
- **They can draw upon a variety of resources in the learning environment, including personal experience, the local community, and the Internet.** For example, the principles of economics become less mysterious when classes enter into a collaborative enterprise with an area radio station to record and market a CD.
- **Their knowledge and understanding are substantively broadened or deepened.** For example, neuroscience becomes less abstract when students use digital imagery to view the workings of the human brain.

Adolescent learning is a complex endeavor, yet current research is clear about the conditions that support it (APA 1997, Lambert and McCombs 1998; McCombs and Whisler 1997; Resnick 1987; 1991, 1999b). Figure 1.2 provides a summary of several broad premises that facilitate adolescent learning.

The current literature on learning and learner-centered practices confirms that many personal, intellectual, and social variables interact within the classroom setting and affect adolescent learning (APA 1997; Bransford et al. 1999; Lambert and McCombs 1998). The broad principles that support an adolescent-centered perspective represent a synthesis of research and theory on teaching and learning (see Figure 1.3).

The Personal Dimension of Learning

Rachel Kessler (2000) in her book, *The Soul of Education: Helping Students Find Connection, Compassion, and Character at School*, described the need for students to feel cared about and connected, to be creative and joyful, to have a sense of purpose, and to believe they can exceed the expectations of others. The personal dimension of adolescent learning encompasses these complex and individualized needs, beliefs, and emotions. Adolescent perceptions about personal ability and effectiveness impact their level of motivation and persistence with new learning tasks. Certain favorable mental "attitudes," such as open-mindedness, tolerance, empathy, and intellectual curiosity, help adolescent thinking to expand and develop at a higher cognitive level. Their learning is enhanced when individual differences are acknowledged,

*Your
Ideas*

Conditions That Support Adolescent Learning

Adolescents learn better when they...

- encounter learning that is appropriate to their developmental level and is presented in multiple ways and in an enjoyable and interesting manner.

- are intellectually intrigued by tasks that are "authentic" and perceived as challenging, novel, and relevant to their own lives.

- are allowed to share and discuss ideas, and to work together on tasks, projects, and problems.

- are afforded multiple strategies to acquire, integrate and interpret knowledge meaningfully, to demonstrate understanding, and to apply knowledge to new situations.

- are provided opportunities to develop and use strategic thinking skills, such as reasoning and problem solving.

- are given guidance and feedback about their work, yet are permitted to monitor personal progress and understanding.

- are in a safe, supportive environment where value is given to personal ideas and negative emotions, such as fear of punishment and embarrassment, are minimized.

Figure 1.2

respected, and accommodated; when students are motivated through challenge, relevance, choice, and a sense of accomplishment; and when they feel comfortable to express, create, explore, experiment, take risks, and make mistakes.

Adolescents' social and emotional well-being is closely linked to what they believe about other peoples' perceptions. Adolescents are inclined to be more conscious of the opinions of those around them, especially their peers. Elkind (1981) referred to the tendency to be preoccupied with what others think as the "imaginary audience" phenomenon. Many adolescents believe that in social situations, all attention is focused on them. As a consequence, they may be overly sensitive. They may react emotionally to kidding, for example, and often hold on to personal feelings of anger or embarrassment. Although students become more socially oriented during the period of adolescence, their perspectives remain predominantly "me centered" and limited.

Adolescent-Centered Teaching

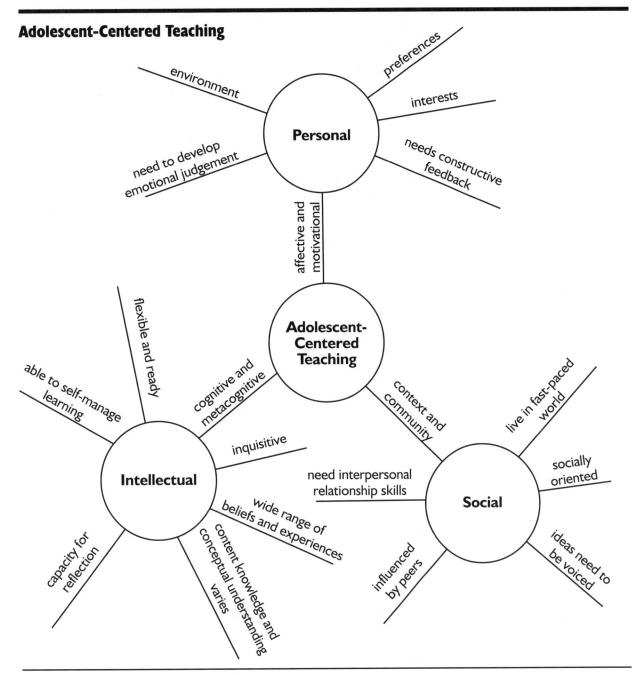

Figure 1.3

Adolescent Motivation

Adolescent motivation is a fascinating and ever-perplexing phenomenon. Adolescents are motivated by what they perceive as personally relevant, and they are aware of their own power, choice, and responsibility. What may be surprising about adolescent motivation is that these young people are naturally motivated to learn—under certain conditions, that is, and when these conditions are personally right.

*Your
Ideas*

Motivation is individual and elusive, important to learning, yet influenced by a person's beliefs, feelings, interests, and goals (Lambert and McCombs 1998). Motivation affects adolescents' willingness to learn and the amount of effort they will exert in the process (Alexander and Murphy 1998). It can be influenced by several factors, which include the following:

- knowledge in a particular content area;
- beliefs about what the teacher expects;
- adolescents' self-concept or perceived personal ability;
- anxiety and concern over grades;
- level of support in the classroom environment;
- difficulty and challenge of the task;
- social interaction; and
- belief that the learning is useful, meaningful, and of consequence for others.

What is challenging about adolescent motivation, however, is that it can vary in intensity and duration among subjects, learning experiences, classrooms, and teachers.

Understanding what motivates adolescents to learn requires paying attention to the interrelated factors that naturally energize and excite them. Strong, Silver, and Robinson (1995) identified four essential goals that drive students' willingness to get involved and to persist in learning experiences. Each goal satisfies an underlying human need that, when satisfied, enables them to deal effectively with the complexities and ambiguities of real life. Adolescents are motivated by (1) success, or need for mastery; (2) curiosity, or need for understanding; (3) originality, or need for self-expression; and (4) relationship, or need for involvement with others in a social context. Teachers are responsive to the basic learning needs that affect adolescent motivation when they do the following:

- engage adolescents through an intriguing curriculum that stimulates their curiosity;
- permit them to express personal and creative ideas;
- allow them to connect with peers and others in a broader community; and
- help them recognize when their work is of high quality and of value to those around them.

Adolescents are naturally curious and intrinsically motivated to find answers to perplexing questions and to find solutions to unresolved problems. Their curiosity is stimulated by tasks that are novel, personally interesting, authentic, and "perceived as worthy by both

adolescents and by the larger society" (Sizer, T. and Sizer, N. 1999, 5).
They have a need to know, yet are more likely to accept the academic
challenge and follow it through to an acceptable completion when they
feel a sense of ownership, accomplishment, and positive relationship
with others in the learning environment (Deci and Ryan 1998).
Competent and autonomous adolescents who are personally and socially confident also tend to be less dependent on external contingencies
such as grades, the approval of others, or the threat of negative consequences (Pintrich and Schrauben 1992).

*Your
Ideas*

    Understanding adolescent motivation is critical in helping them
develop the metacognitive skills for self-directed learning. They
become more self-managing; however, they must first share in the
learning responsibility, which means allowing them input and choice
(Deci and Ryan 1998). In fact, if they are not given some degree of
control in the learning process, they are unlikely to develop the skills
for self-regulation, and may become disinclined to learn at all
(Zimmerman 1994). The complex and powerful phenomenon of adolescent metacognition is addressed later in the chapter.

Teachers Matter

When adolescents are asked what they like best about the classes
where they learn the most, they often begin with the personal traits of
the teacher: "He has a sense of humor." "She is friendly." "He is
patient." "She cares about us." "He always found a way to connect with
every student." Parker Palmer in his highly acclaimed book, The
Courage to Teach, describes teachers who attend to the personal
dimension in this way: "Good teachers possess a capacity for connect-
edness. They are able to weave a complex web of connections among
themselves, their subjects, and their students so that students can learn
to weave a world for themselves" (1998, 11). On a simple level, personal connection with adolescents is made through teacher gestures that
convey interest, caring or thoughtfulness. These small acts might
include

- baking a cake to celebrate a class accomplishment;
- using some Spanish terms to help explain a geometry concept to
  multilingual students; or
- giving students an opportunity to write about their feelings in
  journals.

    On another level, personal connection is made through teacher
actions that give adolescents opportunity and choice. These could
include

*Your
Ideas*

- allowing a highly gifted student to do independent work with more advanced concepts;
- helping students draw relationships between historical events and current events; or
- permitting students to choose the artistic style for a self-portrait assignment.

Attention to adolescents' personal dimensions is important for several reasons. First, this age group needs to be encouraged to develop intellectually and ethically. Adolescence is a formative, tentative, and pivotal time when young people are contemplating significant personal and societal issues. Their ideas may be somewhat confused or misconceived, ill-structured or unrefined, yet they need to feel that their contribution in a discussion matters to the teacher (Sizer, T. and Sizer, N. 1999). Adolescents should be encouraged to share personal perspectives through persuasive writing, interpretive discussion, and creative approaches; to examine their assumptions through opportunities to express, question, and test original ideas; to consider alternatives through debating, role playing, problem solving, or other "encounters" with differing viewpoints, approaches, or solutions; and to think critically about personal decisions and actions by specifying the consequences in a simulated or real context. Adolescents are more likely to take the personal risk involved in letting others know what they are thinking, when they feel accepted, valued, respected, and supported on a personal level.

Adolescents should feel they belong in the classroom community, and they need to develop a sense of empowerment over personal learning management. They are more motivated to learn when they can interact socially and when they are given responsibility (McCombs and Whisler 1997; Ryan 1995; Strong et al. 1995). By the time they reach the teen years, however, adolescents' feelings, beliefs, and self-perceptions have been shaped, negatively and positively, by an assortment of experiences. Understanding the complexity of who they are is no simple matter.

The Intellectual Dimension of Learning

The intellectual dimension centers on adolescents' cognitive readiness for complexity, reflection, and self-regulated learning. This capacity is affected by varying content knowledge, background experiences, and thinking capacities. Cognitively, they are prepared to consider more sophisticated content as they build personal knowledge and further understanding. They are intellectually eager to tackle relevant problems, to discuss pertinent topics, to share viewpoints, and to talk about ethical choices that have implication for their actions. They are ready to use expanding capacities for reasoning, conceptual thinking, and metacognition, and to reflect upon their own thoughts and feelings. They are capable of becoming more responsible and competent in learning management. Adolescent learning is enhanced when students connect new information meaningfully with what they know or have experienced, and this learning is expanded when they acquire and practice metacognitive strategies. Adolescents' learning and cognitive growth is also assisted through ongoing and highly expectant assessment.

Perhaps the cognitive development of adolescents can best be understood through contemporary insight into how they experience learning. Their minds are continually active and flexible. Since an early age, they have gathered knowledge, organized information, and solved problems in an effort to make sense of what was occurring in their lives (Bransford et al. 1999). Though not as stage-discrete and age-bound as Piaget (1928) originally proposed, adolescent cognitive development can be viewed as a progression of knowledge acquisition that has been, and continues to be, shaped through interaction with others and with their environment.

Adolescents have the capacity to reason and think abstractly about knowledge that is familiar or meaningful to them, yet when ideas are new or disconnected to what they know, their thinking appears somewhat concrete. Since they have had the opportunity to acquire more knowledge in general than younger students, they deal more successfully with hypothetical situations. They explain their reasoning better and can recognize more readily instances of illogical thinking (Ormond 1999). Adolescents also tend to show an increasing capability to focus their attention over a longer period of time. They more quickly integrate new information with what they have previously learned, and they are more skilled at drawing relationships among concepts and ideas (Flavell 1985). Schurr (1989, 23) has identified several intellectual content-related capacities of the adolescent. These cognitive capabilities and the implication for adolescent learning are outlined in Figure 1.4.

Adolescents also have a more developed aptitude for metacognition. This intellectual capacity enables them to evaluate the quality of their thinking, to develop a flexible repertoire of thinking and learning strategies, and to decide which strategies to use in certain learning situations. This capacity additionally enables adolescents to reflect upon and more fully understand personal feelings and emotions. In many adolescents, however, the regions of their brains that are responsible for judgment, insight, and planning are yet to be developed (Begley 2000).

Your Ideas

KWL

Cognitive Capabilities and Implication

Intellectual Capacities	Instructional Implication
Appreciation for mathematical logic	Complex problems that invite reasoning and alternate approaches Opportunity to explain logic
Analysis of political ideology	Comparative analysis and critique of varying government systems or cultures
Understanding of the nuances of poetic metaphor and musical notation	Interpretive analyses of literary works where meaning is not readily explicit
Interpretation of symbols, concepts, themes, sayings, and generalizations	An emphasis on broad, abstract ideas and their implication vs. less significant facts
Propositional thinking and deductive reasoning	Opportunities to generate hypotheses, test assumptions, reason through findings, and generate solutions to problems or problem situations

Figure 1.4

Metacognition can afford the intellectual power to assess reactions in situations, to control impulsiveness and temper negative emotions, to think about the consequence of personal decisions, and to act with healthy judgment in social situations.

Metacognition as Personal Power

The intellectual process of metacognition has received much attention recently as a component of good thinking management (Paris and Winograd 1990; Tishman et al. 1995). Metacognition is recognized as a powerful phenomenon that enables students to set goals, plan, problem solve, monitor progress, and evaluate their own thinking effectiveness. It gives adolescents awareness and control over personal thinking behavior, and enables self-reflection and self-regulation (Costa 1991; Fogarty 1995). It provides the means for adolescents to oversee thinking as it happens, to determine what they know, to appraise what they need to know, and to orchestrate what they should do in a learning situation. Sizer described the metacognitive adolescent as "a mindful student . . . who knows where he [or she] is going, is disposed to get there, and is gathering the resources, the knowledge, and the skills to make the journey" (1992, 27). This person generally feels personally competent, autonomous, and socially adept.

Cueing Questions

Metacognition has the capacity to "cultivate cognitive resourceful-ness . . . promote responsible and independent thinking . . . [and]foster strategic thinking and planfulness" (Tishman et al. 1995, 68). It gives adolescents the mental tools for self-directed learning. Barry Beyer (1987) suggested that teachers ask purposeful cueing questions to prompt metacognitive thinking in adolescents. Examples follow.

- When a student is involved in an academic task, a teacher might ask, What are you trying to do?, to elicit the purpose for a chosen approach.
- A question such as, Why are you doing it?, shifts the student's thinking to rationale.
- Is there another way you might do it? encourages a consideration of alternate strategies and supports flexible thinking.
- At the completion of a task, a teacher can promote metacognitive reflection and evaluation with the questions, How well did it work? or Is there a better way?
- The query, How can you help someone else do it?, reinforces learning and challenges the student to discuss possible strategies with another.

Levels of Metacognition

Swartz and Perkins (1989) distinguished four levels of metacogni-tion—tacit, aware, strategic, and reflective. Many adolescents operate on the tacit, or automatic use level. They go through the "right" think-ing processes without giving much thought as to why. On the aware level, adolescents are conscious of their thinking, and on the strategic level, they begin to organize their thinking based on an acknowledged strategy. Ultimately, on the reflective level, adolescents continually assess their strategies and evaluate when and how these can be improved. Functioning at the reflective level indicates greater aware-ness and personal control over thinking at the beginning, middle, and the completion of the learning activity.

Teachers can encourage the development of metacognition in ado-lescent learners. Current ideas about strategic thinking and mental management indicate several instructional elements that facilitate the process. The initial step is to make adolescents aware of their personal metacognitive power and help them to realize that they can develop strategies that are useful and appropriate for learning situations. Teachers can use check questioning to keep the students on the expect-ed "mental track." They can ask for the rationale behind their decisions; remind them of necessary steps to consider; arrange for self-evaluation;

Your Ideas

1 – tacit
2 – awareness
3 – strategic
4 – reflective

*Your
Ideas*

and give students general feedback and support. Teachers encourage reflective metacognition through the following actions:

- Discuss the usefulness of students' strategies in organizing for a presentation;
- Have them write about their thought processes in a response journal;
- Ask them explain their planning strategies to other students; and
- Help them to identify strategies they might use in real life situations.

Scholars and researchers, including Barell (1995), Costa (1991), Daniels and Bizar (1998), Fogarty (1995), Palincsar and Brown (1984), Paris and Winograd (1990), Tishman et al. (1995) have suggested several instructional techniques that foster metacognitive skills. These include role playing and simulation, journal keeping, problem solving, reciprocal teaching, cognitive coaching, modeling, direct explanation, elaboration, self-questioning, self-assessment, reflection, and planning strategies that emphasize thinking before, during, and after a thinking challenge.

The following Adolescent-Centered Teaching (ACT) Model is an example of the way teachers might promote adolescent metacognitive development. It is based on an instructional technique called the "Mystery Strategy" in which students are confronted with a challenging, realistic event (Geocaris 1997, 73; Silver and Hanson 1994). Students are actively involved as they organize a set of given clues, formulate and test hypotheses, and propose probable explanations. The process ends with a reflection stage in which students evaluate the effectiveness of their investigation. The strategy involves rigor, thoughtful inquiry, and opportunity for originality and creativity. The adolescents also learn to think as scientists as they inquire, analyze data, make predictions, and build understanding.

Promoting Metacognitive Development: Dr. DNA

Adolescents are intrigued by realistic and puzzling phenomena that stimulate their curiosity and challenge their thinking. Complex content and ideas can be presented in an authentic format that engages problem-solving skills, allows for choice and creative expression, and promotes metacognitive reflection. The teacher's role is to help students to develop strategies for learning, to ask for rationale, to give feedback, to encourage self-monitoring, and to help them extend the learning into real life situations.

Content Understanding

Teachers should consider the essential understanding of the discipline and the pertinent state and national curriculum standards. Goals should be set accordingly.

- ■ To help adolescents discern the relationship among DNA, RNA, proteins, and genetics and to develop skills for scientific inquiry and problem solving.

ESSENTIAL QUESTION

What is DNA and how does it contribute to genetics and life diversity?

Strategies for Inquiry

Adolescents are motivated and challenged by authentic and intriguing events, problems, and questions. Teachers should consider ways to stimulate their curiosity to explore, investigate, and solve.

The Inquiry Event: Dr. DNA, a renowned microbiologist and geneticist, was scheduled to present important findings on the causes of diversity in living organisms at an international science symposium. While crossing a busy intersection on the way to the convention center, Dr. DNA was struck by a speeding van and killed. Valuable research notes were scattered at the accident scene. The National Science Foundation has assembled a group of scientists to reconstruct Dr. DNA's theory from the retrieved papers. You (the student) have been chosen to join this important team.

Guided Interaction

Teachers need to guide as adolescents set up strategies for inquiry and as they proceed through learning tasks. While the teacher's role is continually active, it should become less directive as the experience progresses.

- ◼ Teachers should develop clues (without explanation) based on important ideas and concepts about DNA, type these on separate paper strips, and distribute them to student teams.
- ◼ Students should look for patterns in the random clues (ostensibly Dr. DNA's research papers) as they manipulate and sort them into categories. In analyzing the data, students can consult relevant sources, such as their textbook, the Internet, and the teacher, as they attempt to develop an explanation of DNA.

Metacognitive Reflection and Assessment

This phase is the most critical for adolescent intellectual development. Teachers need to structure time for assessment of and reflection on the learning. Students should be actively involved in setting criteria, in evaluating performance, and in extending learning to other settings.

- ◼ Students can use team journals to record their questions, observations, and thought processes. Teachers should periodically ask that these be shared and discussed.

■ Teams will prepare an oral report for a simulated research symposium as a final product. They might develop visuals and design programs. The simulated research symposium can be conducted online in conjunction with other schools in the district, county, state, or even country.

■ Teachers and students will work together to develop evaluation criteria based on content (understanding of concepts related to theory), critical thinking (ability to analyze data and construct explanations), and communication (ability to present findings in a clear manner).

■ During the final performance assessment (simulation), teachers should ask for clarification and elaboration, and other students should have an opportunity to give feedback on the reasonableness of the teams' explanations.

■ As a final reflection, teachers and adolescents need to discuss the often real-world expectation to make sense of situations based on given evidence: They might also reflect on their level of motivation during the process, how effectively they managed the inquiry, the value of writing out and verbalizing their thinking, the usefulness of sharing ideas, and what they understand better about their own thinking and learning.

Cross-Disciplinary Applications

■ In English, a teacher might read aloud to students sequential passages of an intriguing story, such as Roald Dahl's "The Landlady," and have students predict, using the B.E.T. strategy (Based on clues," Estimate the Possibilities," and "Tender your BET!"), what could happen next based on the clues rendered. They should explain their reasoning during the predictions and reflect upon it at the end.

■ A social studies application could be an exchange of clues among students in two different parts of the country or world to locate each other. Clues should give ideas about location, climate, industry and other demographics.

*Your
Ideas*

The Social Dimension of Learning

Adolescents have a strong need to belong and to be accepted in and out of school. They actively seek to determine their role and status in the broader social order. They deal intentionally with the search for personal identity and often adopt different ones in the uncertainty of who they are becoming (Ormond 1999). Placing a great deal of energy into how they present themselves to others, adolescents may insist on a certain hairstyle or a certain brand of clothing or they may align themselves in other visible ways with a particular peer group. Conformity often serves as a mask, or safe personae, that provides respite amidst the many changes in their lives. Although adolescents test personal limits and push fiercely for independence, they simultaneously seek the security of being socially affiliated and individually less obvious.

An instructional environment that is responsive to the social dimension of adolescent learning provides structured opportunities for peer interaction, yet within this context, high expectations must be set for individual respect and tolerance. A sense of community is promoted when adolescents feel personally valued and accepted. Chapter 3 deals further with the important role of the classroom environment in adolescent learning and personal, intellectual, and social development. Figure 1.5 summarizes adolescents' personal, intellectual, and social characteristics, and correlates several related learning needs.

By The Time They Reach Adolescence...

Adolescents have a fairly good idea of what they can and cannot learn—or at least what they think they can. Heredity, past experiences, other people, and previous learning have shaped them, cognitively, emotionally and socially. Positive or negative, each encounter has contributed in some way to what they believe to be true about themselves (Lambert and McCombs 1998). Being female, for example, may be linked to lack of academic confidence in a particular subject area, such as math or science. This association may be reinforced by societal expectations or personal embarrassment and frustration. The cumulative interaction of numerous other factors, including the congruence with teaching styles, the level of family support, diversity in culture and language, or variations in aptitude, knowledge, skills and interest, affect adolescents' beliefs about themselves and their individual learning competence. Adolescents' internal reality systems function much like a lens through which experiences (academic, social, and personal) in and out of school, are viewed (McCombs and Whisler 1997). How confident, worthy, or capable they feel can influence how they negotiate new learning experi-

Adolescent Developmental Tendencies and Implications for Learning

Personal	Learning Needs
Anxious for developmental normality	Climate of acceptance, tolerance
Easily angered, slow to recover	Emotional safety, guidance
Push for independence, autonomy	Choice, responsibility, accountability
Easily discouraged if do not achieve	Appropriate challenge, relative success

Intellectual	Learning Needs
Have diverse knowledge, interests, abilities	Opportunities to develop range of skill and to pursue variety of content areas
Can see relationships among similar concepts, ideas, and experiences	Complex subject matter, relevant issues
Capable of inferential thinking, reasoning	Higher-level, analytical questioning
Capable of critical evaluation, extended focus	Time and opportunity for critical thinking
Reflective, metacognitive, self-motivated	Self-evaluation, choice

Social	Learning Needs
Can be indifferent to adult figures	Opportunity to interact with knowledgeable adults in collaborative projects
Concerned about self-presentation to peers	Emphasis on cooperation, inclusiveness, group contribution
Strive to conform for peer acceptance	Structured, positive student interaction

Figure 1.5

ences. When past learning encounters have been consistently negative in a particular area, adolescents tend to be less confident in their abilities to succeed in related learning situations (Bandura 1993). When adolescents believe in their own learning capabilities, however, and have the adequate knowledge or skill base, they tend to "participate more readily, work harder, and persist longer even when they encounter difficulties" (Schunk 1994, 79).

Your Ideas

Adolescents' self-views are tied closely to what they believe about their own competence and ability, and the level of control they think they have to manage the effort needed to accomplish a task. These perceptions can vary from subject to subject, and may facilitate or impede their motivation, performance, and achievement. When students experience success after having exerted some level of individual effort, they more often attribute the accomplishment to their personal ability and hard work. Their confidence (self-efficacy) is enhanced, allowing them to regulate and manage their own learning to greater effect.

Self-Efficacy

Adolescents' social, personal, and cognitive experiences interact and affect their perceptions and learning behavior. This complex phenomenon can be explained in part by current social cognitive research. Bandura (1993) described self-efficacy as perceived beliefs about one's capability to learn in a particular area or to perform at an expected level. These beliefs affect how motivated adolescents are to try a particular task, how much effort they will put into it, and how much control they feel they have to complete the task successfully. Theorists believe that adolescents who are "efficacious" are more inclined to set personal learning goals, to determine and take advantage of available resources, to choose appropriate personal learning strategies, and to monitor their own learning progress (Zimmerman 1994).

Social-cognitive educators urge that classroom experiences be structured in ways that help adolescents develop a stronger sense of personal competence and assume a more proactive role in their own learning management (Ames 1992; Schunk 1994). As adolescents strengthen affective, cognitive, and metacognitive skills, they gain the self-efficacy that is foundational for self-regulated learning. Several suggested strategies that promote self-efficacy follow:

- **Enable adolescents to feel a sense of accomplishment on tasks that challenge their thinking and effort.** A teacher might allow students to select a research topic of personal interest. Two students who select genetic engineering, for example, could interview a biotechnology expert at the university. They could design graphics, download a video clip of "Dolly" for a multimedia presentation, and lead a class debate on the ethics of cloning.

- **Teach them to set realistic learning goals and help them acquire strategies that best attain these goals.** The teacher in the above example would assist as the students plan their research strategy. Guiding questions might include, What do you need to find out about genetic engineering? Where is the expertise and how can it be tapped? What are the pertinent resources? What are the goals for the presentation? What assistance do you need? What can you manage on your own?

Your Ideas

- **Encourage them to attribute their success to their own ability and hard work.** By permitting "guided" self-direction, teachers can help adolescents begin to manage their learning. The science students assume responsibility for carrying out the research project, yet they are mindful of when and how to seek assistance. Teachers help adolescents feel the satisfaction of personal accomplishment when they allow and acknowledge students' initiative, creativity, and achievement.

- **Help them pay attention to which strategies work best for them personally in certain situations.** Teachers should monitor adolescents' learning activity closely, and advise that they recognize and alter a strategy that is not effective. A time to "step back" and reflect on the process is important. Following the research presentation, for example, the students should evaluate their plan. Did the interview with the college professor extend their knowledge? What did they gain by "stretching" their technology skills? Will they seek the help of outside experts in future assignments? How does the sharing of knowledge benefit learning?

The Paradox of Puberty

Almost two decades ago, Sizer (1984, 33) characterized adolescence in appropriately paradoxical language:

> Besides their age, they have in common the vulnerability that comes with inexperience and a social status bordering on limbo. They are children, but they are adults, too. Many are ready and able to work, but are dissuaded from doing so. They can bear children, but are counseled not to. They can kill, and sometimes do. They can act autonomously but are told what to do . . . They share the pain of a stereotype, of gum-chewing, noisy, careless, bloomingly sexual creatures who are allowed to have fun but not too much of it.

The tension in the period between puberty and young adulthood is even more apparent today as adolescents encounter a world defined by increasing complexity and expectation. Theirs is a time when condoms are dispensed in school-based clinics and personal lives are shaped by a culture far more sophisticated than the experiences in their classrooms. Too often, however, their cognitive capacity for understanding goes underestimated and their motivation to take responsibility for their own learning consequently diminishes. Understanding adolescents as learners and *thinkers* is imperative.

ACTing
on the Adolescent-Centered Learning
Principles Discussed in Chapter 1

Principle	*How I can put it into practice*
❏ Recognize that internal and external factors affect adolescent thinking and learning.	
❏ Acknowledge the personal, intellectual, and social needs of the adolescent learner.	
❏ Recognize that adolescents are developmentally ready for empathy, understanding, reflection, and intellectual engagement.	
❏ Don't underestimate the cognitive and metacognitive capacity of adolescents.	
❏ Create challenge that is appropriate to their level of knowledge, skill and development, and provide opportunity for in-depth understanding and meaningful interaction.	
❏ Structure lessons that allow for student choice and appropriately-guided autonomy.	

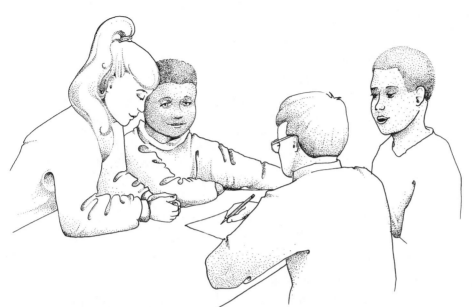

We're Losing Their Attention

Recognizing the Need to Connect

The culture of secondary schools has changed minimally over the past few decades. Bands still practice on school lawns and parking lots, and pep rallies shorten Friday morning's schedule. Banners touting athletic championships remain prominently draped over glassed trophy cases in gymnasium foyers, and the distinctive smell of cafeteria food permeates the air by mid-morning. Displays of blue-ribboned artwork celebrate student achievement, and colorful posters promote upcoming choral events. The clang of lockers echoes the length of hallways, and student voices are quelled with the fading ring of the second bell. Classroom doors close upon rows of students, and teachers begin to talk.

In many ways, the students behind these classroom doors are themselves timelessly familiar. They experiment with new styles, chatter about music and movies, complain about homework, test the patience of parents and teachers, and generally succeed at hiding their insecurities. They change their minds and change their moods in a predictably unpredictable manner. More than at any point in their lives,

Your Ideas

they are conscious of their appearance, and of how others perceive them. They try out ideas and try on identities; they negotiate personal confidence and explore new ways of thinking. At times with awkward steps and at other times with swaggering strides, these youth are tentatively and tenaciously traversing the middle ground between pre-adolescence and young adulthood.

A closer look into the classrooms, however, reveals a new adolescent, and the implication for what and how they are taught is drawing considerable attention. These youths are more diverse, more sophisticated, and simultaneously more vulnerable than those in previous generations. New technologies have expanded their world, and vicariously through media or directly through experience, they have been exposed early to a society that leaves little room for innocence. Violence has entered their classrooms and the perpetrators are their own peers. An uneasy security of metal detectors, conflict mediation initiatives, and personal sanctions pervades their school environment. In addition, beyond the immediacy of their daily circumstance, these adolescents face a future in which the command of content knowledge, critical thinking, and the skills for self-directed learning and interpersonal relationships will be necessary for the workplace and important to the quality of their adult lives.

A New Adolescent

The current generation of youth brings a distinctive set of experiences into the classroom and a new set of challenges for teachers. Their social, emotional, and intellectual development has been shaped and continues to be influenced by access and exposure. Technology and media determine the way they acquire both information and attitude. The Internet alone has had substantial impact on adolescent consciousness, providing a seemingly limitless, instantaneous, and often unqualified resource of information. It is not surprising that adolescents perceive many traditional instructional tools outdated and much of the curriculum boring and disconnected from their personal lives.

Culturally, ethnically, and linguistically diverse, many adolescents have been exposed directly to physical violence and others deal daily with adult-sized concerns. While most are enticed, many have been lured successfully by a drug culture that pervades the society around them. While many adolescents' experiences have included preschool, summer camp, and travel, an astounding number, in what Sizer (1996) has referred to as the "new American poverty," have been left without health care, home stability, or any semblance of financial security. Their family configurations vary from nuclear to single-parent to blended.

Their caretakers, for the most part, work full-time outside the home, leaving adolescents in charge of younger siblings in the afternoon. More so than in the last half-century, for varying reasons, the experiences of young people have left them with "a sense of being on their own" (1996, 25). Of all the issues that trouble them, loneliness ranks highest (Kantrowitz and Wingert 1999).

Your Ideas

While a number of adolescents become "disenfranchised" with their school experiences and drop out; more so than in the past twenty years, students are staying in school (O'Brien et al. 1997; Resnick 1999). More are selecting academic programs, completing graduation requirements, and attending some form of college (Codding and Rothman 1999). More aspire to professional careers, compete for scholarships, and worry over making the right decisions about their future. More seem to recognize the advantage of post-secondary education and the uncertainty of the job market (Schneider and Stevenson 1999).

Preparing for a Demanding Future

The need to prepare adolescents for what lies ahead is critical, for their future will be emphatically different. In his recent book, *The Disciplined Mind: What All Students Should Understand*, Howard Gardner described the importance of educating today's students for a world that has changed dramatically and is continuing to change rapidly: "I envision a world citizenry that is highly literate, disciplined, capable of thinking critically and creatively, knowledgeable about a range of cultures, able to participate actively in discussions about new discoveries and choices, willing to take risks for what it believes in" (1999, 25).

What continues to dismay educators, however, is that a large number of high school graduates remember or understand little of what they supposedly learned and do not think effectively about what they can recall or believe they do know (Gardner 1999; Perkins 1992; Wiggins and McTigue 1998). They continue to lag behind twelfth graders internationally in pertinent areas such as reading, mathematics, and science (Codding and Rothman 1999). According to Resnick's assessment, "[O]ur population today is not really better educated, despite the dramatic increase over the years of the proportion of students who complete high school" (1999a, *x*). Many educators have begun to question the value of school experiences to prepare adolescents realistically for the rigor of post-secondary education or for the complexity of adult living (Codding and Rothman 1999; Gibbs 1999).

What is equally distressing is that a number of adolescents perceive little connection between the learning experiences in schools and what is important in the world beyond the classroom. They remain in

Your Ideas

school "simply to get their tickets punched and get on with their lives" (Codding and Rothman 1999, 5). Many assume a "just passing through" attitude, while others express specific concerns about how they are taught. In spite of a vigorous and pervasive movement toward higher standards, the academic expectations in many classrooms are far below what students are capable of knowing and achieving, and what they will need to know for subsequent schooling and productive adult lives. Figure 2.1 summarizes the "disconnect" between students' aspirations and expectations and their educational experience.

We're Losing Their Attention

A Different Set of Expectations...   **A Growing Disconnect...**

Increased Selection of
More Academic Courses   Limited Rigor in Preparation
                                         Trailing International Test Scores

Higher Graduation Rate   A Curriculum of Diminishing Relevance to
                                         Experiences

More Exposure and Access   Traditional Instructional Delivery

Greater Opportunity for   "Fragile" Knowledge
Higher Education   Underdeveloped Thinking Capacity

Concerns About Preparation   Lowered Expectations for Academic
For College   Performance

Heightened Career Aspirations   Unpracticed in Decision-Making
                                         and Collaboration Skills

Greater Potential for the Future   Limited Potential for Professional
                                         Contribution

Figure 2.1

Figure 2.2 profiles the complex personal, social, and intellectual characteristics of today's adolescent. These needs are further elaborated in the following sections.

The Challenge is Clear

Teaching adolescents effectively calls for a better understanding of who they are, how they feel, and what motivates them to think and to learn.

A Profile of Today's Adolescent

May Be...	Yet May...
Technological "Savvy"	Lack skill to organize, evaluate, synthesize data
Multicultural, Multilingual	Feel stymied by one culture's ideas and language
Used to Fast Access	Lack motivation to persevere for task completion
Socially Active	Lack the skills for purposeful social interaction
Peer Oriented	Need assistance with interpersonal relationship
Intellectually Capable	Be unpracticed in higher cognitive thinking
Future Oriented	Lack the skills for self-management and regulation
Exposed to Experience	Struggle with moral judgment and ethical decisions
Information-Rich	Be limited in opportunity to explore broader issues
Independent-Minded	Be personally vulnerable to peer and societal lure
College/Work-Bound	Be limited in content and practical knowledge

Figure 2.2

The demands of their future are also equally apparent. Whether for college or a higher-skilled job, they will need sound knowledge, a critical mind, the ability to relate to others, and the capacity to know how to continue their learning (Tucker and Codding 1999). Teachers must structure a learning environment responsive to the intellectual, personal, and social needs of this new generation of adolescents—a clear and nonnegotiable challenge.

The New Geography of Learning

Adolescents are far more influenced by the world beyond the classroom than students in recent decades. They can observe a full solar eclipse transmitted from a prime vantage in the Middle East simply by visiting an Internet site. They can view an online exhibition in the Egyptian Museum in Cairo, post questions on instant message centers, contribute ideas to youth forums, and "chat" with other young people throughout the world. "[T]he geography of learning stretches far

*Your
Ideas*

beyond the physical space of the school (Hargreaves 1997, 4), and the walls of the traditional classroom no longer hold a monopoly on adolescents' learning experiences. Consequently, teachers cannot expect the student to be satisfied with instructional strategies that limit them to the immediate physical context.

Adolescents' reality is defined by speed, color, sound, and movement, and data comes easily and quickly to their fingertips. Fast-paced interactive video games have long challenged their mental acuity and dexterity, and terminology such as "surf," "synchronous," and "virtual" is common vernacular. They track rock group concerts, watch movies, shop, create Web pages, upload data files, and download music with a few taps on the home computer keyboard. New technologies have literally transformed the way adolescents acquire information and communicate with one another. Their world is one of digital imagery, graphic simulation, and global connection.

Although technology is not a panacea for education's ills, it is hard not to recognize the power of databases to collect and manipulate pertinent information; of digital libraries to facilitate research; of videodisks to enhance problem solving; of simulations to help visualize concepts; and of personal computers to compose, draw, diagram, image, or communicate limitlessly (Gardner 1999). Technology brings real-world problems into the classroom for adolescents to explore, and it connects them with others in a networked knowledge-building community. Its interactive capability provides feedback about the quality of their thinking and enables reflection and revision (Bransford, Brown, and Cocking 1999). Technology also enables adolescents to learn to analyze, synthesize, and make more informed judgments about the vast amount of information so readily available. The ACT Model, "The Information Challenge," illustrates a way to help adolescents learn to evaluate the vast amount of information so readily available.

The Information Challenge: Deceived By The Truth?

Adolescents are bombarded with advertisements and luring messages on the Internet, television, radio, audio, and print sources, such as billboards and newspapers. The commercial market has targeted them through emotional appeal and persuasion in the areas of music, fashion, sports, entertainment, and pseudo-sophisticated lifestyles. The challenge to youth is to sort through the marketing blitz, recognize the method of attraction, and determine fact from fiction or embellishment. At times, they may have to realize that even the truth can be deceiving. This thematic unit focuses on the impact of commercialism on adolescents' social, emotional, and intellectual development.

Content Understanding

Theme: Commercialism

Interdisciplinary: To help adolescents learn to evaluate the print and non-print communication for bias, sensationalism, and advertising appeal and to apply the skills of statistical data analysis and decision making as potential consumers.

Technology: To provide opportunities for adolescents to use technologies to access, analyze, interpret, synthesize, apply, and communicate information.

ESSENTIAL QUESTION

How does commercialism affect the lives of teens?

Strategies for Inquiry

Precipitating Question: If you wanted to market a product to your peers, what techniques would you use to make it appeal to them?

Teachers might ask students to consider the following challenge:

> Ongoing allegations by consumers against large tobacco companies have resulted in multi-million dollar fines and judgments.

■ Do you think these are justified?

■ Should consumers be more responsible for their actions?

■ Would your ideas change in any way if you were told that a high percentage of smokers begin smoking before the age of twelve?

■ What if you found out that many cigarette machines were intentionally placed near middle schools?

■ How do you feel about the use of cartoon figures in tobacco ads?

Teachers could show a popular television commercial and have students critique the appeal to the adolescent market.

Guided Inquiry

■ In language arts, students can view videotapes of popular "infomercials" (exercise programs, skin products, sports equipment) and other advertisements on the Internet, television, or in print. Guiding questions might include the followig: What is the emotional appeal? What tactics are used? Who is the targeted audience? Why? Where are any discrepancies or use of generalizations? How are testimonials used? What statistics are used? Are they valid? In small groups students can discuss the validity of the information and discern rationale for consumer appeal.

■ In social studies, during a study of apartheid, students can analyze advertisements that perpetuate stereotyping of African culture.

■ In science, during a study of genetics, students can use the scientific method to explore the sensationalism of tabloids and Internet sites.

■ In math, students can calculate the discrepancies in food labels and advertisement or use statistical knowledge and online consumer reports to determine the best car deal.

Metacognitive Development and Assessment

Teachers can pose extension questions that promote reflection on observations, such as

■ If testimonials, surveys, and statistical reports are truthful, how might they misrepresent the truth? (personal bias, non-random and non-representative sampling, anecdotal testimonials)

■ How do ads target certain audiences? (billboard location, Internet games, music Web sites, television and radio time slots)

■ What makes advertising truthful? How can the accuracy be checked?

■ Why is emotional appeal more effective? Can there be a balance, e.g., truth and strategic appeal?

Student understanding can be assessed through various content products. These might include

- a language arts persuasive paper on the effect of commercialism on them and society;
- a social studies advertisement to attract new British settlers to South Africa in the 1770s;
- a role play to promote a new scientific advancement in cell theory; and
- a statistical analysis report of the truthfulness in advertising of food companies.

As a culminating assessment, teams of students might create a multimedia commercial to promote an original product. Within groups, students can assume various roles, including commercial designer, product designer, reporter, money manager, or research manufacturer. Teachers should serve as advisors for each role and a "loan" could be extended for product and commercial development.

Evaluation criteria for the final presentation might include

- targeted audience appeal,
- accuracy of information,
- strategic (yet "truthful") persuasiveness, and
- appropriateness of technology (graphics, audio enhancement).

Helpful Online Resources for this ACT

Consumer Reports.
http://www.consumerreports.org.
Corporate Watch
http://www.corpwatch.org/
Federal Consumer Information Center.
http://www.pueblo.gsa.gov/
Federal Trade Commission. http://www.ftc.gov
Weekly World News Online
http://www.weeklyworldnews.com

Cross-Disciplinary Applications

- In English, in preparation for a research paper, adolescents might evaluate the credibility of Web sites for information.

- In science students might interview NASA scientists (online) to check the validity of regional newspapers in reporting coverage of ongoing missions.

Web site research courtesy of E. Crowell, A. Peoples-Robinson, M. Swanik, (May 2000). Elon College, North Carolina.

*Your
Ideas*

Additionally, adolescents face a world where complex ethical issues vie for their attention. Human cloning and genetic engineering define the landscape of biotechnology; international peace is negotiated with chemical warfare; and medical advancement competes with cultural preservation. Students struggle regularly with moral decisions and social actions, and society puzzles over the motivation behind teen violence. By contrast, the classroom learning experiences are frequently dictated by a curriculum that puts heavy emphasis on textbook knowledge, definitive solutions, and predictable steps. The pressure of end-of-course tests and advanced-placement examinations have forced many teachers to cover information so rapidly that the opportunity to delve into meaningful content issues is limited. Opportunities to think conceptually about the significant ideas that endure beyond the classroom experience are often minimal (Wiggins and McTigue 1998; Sizer, T. and Sizer, N. 1999). Regardless of the circumstance, the need to deal with matters of greater significance remains in adolescents' lives.

One pervasive factor that may contribute to the widening gap between adolescents' learning needs and their school experiences is a limited understanding by teachers of the conditions that facilitate learning. Learning is a natural, interactive, and emotionally-charged process of knowledge construction (Resnick 1999b). It requires teachers to make an intentional connection with what adolescents know, feel, and believe. It is enhanced when students are actively involved, when they are able to relate meaningfully to new information, and when they feel personally valued and successful (McCombs and Whisler 1997). Learning is also strengthened when adolescents work together with a common purpose, and when they are given feedback about the quality of their work. Because learning is closely tied to the particular situation of the instructional experience, it is additionally more enduring when the context is realistic and relevant to students' lives.

Learning is also directly connected to adolescent motivation. As Gardner eloquently explained: "If one is motivated to learn, one is likely to work hard, to be persistent, to be stimulated rather than discouraged by obstacles, and to continue to learn even when not pressed to do so, for the sheer pleasure of quenching curiosity or stretching one's faculties in unfamiliar directions" (1999, 76). Learning is stimulated by complexity and challenge, the lack of which generally causes boredom (Strong, Silver, and Robinson 1995). An expectation for thoughtful learning and the genuine understanding of intricate content, however, is not as widespread as it should be (Gardner 1991, 1999; Sizer 1996; Wiggins and McTigue 1998). This tendency to underestimate adolescents' potential to deal with content in a meaningful and thoughtful way is addressed in the following section.

In the Valley of Low Expectations

Setting expectations too low may be linked to an underestimation of adolescents' capabilities. There might be the fear that struggling students will "give up" under the pressure to work harder or if they are expected to put more thought and energy into an assignment. Teachers may think that some adolescents lack the background experience, knowledge, or ability to handle a complex task. The more rigorous academic expectations might be reserved for the brighter students, although, unfortunately, even America's top-ranked students could be better challenged (U.S. Department of Education 1996). In some instances, the climate of the entire school revolves around the philosophy that adolescents should not be pushed too hard academically and that their educational experiences should be the last safe haven "before the world turns serious on them" (Gibbs 1999, 70).

Grappling

For whatever reason, expectations are often set lower than what adolescents can handle. They are frequently given limited opportunity to wrestle mentally with substantive subject matter. In their recent book, *The Students Are Watching: Schools and the Moral Contract* (Sizer, T. and Sizer, N. 1999), the authors use the term "grappling" to denote the process of striving to know important content on a level that reflects true understanding. Grappling involves the discussion of content-related issues and problems pertinent to the ongoing experiences of adolescents. Grappling also assumes that these students have something meaningful to contribute, such as relevant knowledge or ventured opinions. Because adolescents are considering, questioning, and formulating beliefs that will affect their decisions, they should be encouraged to express them so their thoughts can be developed, refined, and strengthened. To underestimate what adolescents have to offer or to believe that a certain level of thinking is beyond them is expecting too little.

Content of Consequence

Challenging adolescents to think more deeply about content begins with a look at the content itself. In many instances, adolescents are asked to "learn" content that lacks purpose, relevance, connection, or meaningfulness to what they know, can relate to, or have experienced. Also, rather than stimulating and challenging adolescents' intellectual curiosity about important content issues, teachers often merely tell students what they need to know. They do not allow for meaningful inter-action with the content. Those who teach with the adolescent brain in mind use the following questions when making curricular and instructional decisions:

- Has time been allotted to identify the important knowledge, including facts, concepts and principles, or the essential understandings of a discipline?
- Is the content too broad, too unconnected or too prescriptive, in what has been referred to as "broad-brush knowledge"? (Wiggins and McTigue 1998, 9)
- Has consideration been given to what is known and is familiar to adolescents?
- Has thought been given to the manner in which students can be intrigued and actively involved?
- Have students been encouraged to question or speculate?
- Will they be allowed to simulate, debate, discuss, reflect, or err?

For a number of years educators have been concerned that students' practical understanding of pertinent concepts and underlying principles is limited (Gardner 1991; 1999; Resnick 1989, 1999b; Sizer 1996; Sizer T. and Sizer, N. 1999). David Perkins in his book, *Smart Schools: From Training Memories to Educating Minds*, wrote of a shortfall in students' ability to retain, apply, and use knowledge in a way that helps them to benefit and understand their world. He described this knowledge as "fragile" in terms of it being incomplete, misconceived, ritualistic, or even simply retained long enough for a test (1992, 26). Adolescents may have simplistic theories about scientific principles or mathematical concepts. They may lack knowledge about geographical location, be confused about historical phenomena, or be too literal in interpretation. They may also cling to stereotypical perceptions of culture, race, or ethnicity.

Not confined to a particular discipline, fragile knowledge is perpetuated when information is simply added on, rather than connected to what students already know. Perkins urged teachers to structure learning experiences where students are challenged to "learn about and think with what they are learning" (1992, 8). In his 1933 book, *How We Think*, John Dewey expressed early dismay for an education system that viewed young people as passive recipients in the learning process. His continuing concern for the detrimental effect of education that does not focus on students and their learning is evident in the questions he raises in a later book, *Experience and Education* (1938, 26–27):

How many students . . . were rendered callous to ideas, and how
many lost the impetus to learn because of the way in which learning
was experienced by them? How many acquired special skills by
means of automatic drill so that their power of judgment and capacity to act intelligently in new situations was limited? How many
came to associate the learning process with ennui and boredom?
How many found what they did learn so foreign to the situations of
life outside the school as to give them no power of control over the
latter?

Your Ideas

These questions hold timeless pertinence as the classroom conditions that challenge and support the adolescent thinking and learning
become more prevalent.

A Safe Place to Learn

Undeniably, adolescence is a tumultuous time. Spanning the years
between late childhood and young adulthood, it is a period when students' thoughts are more socially than academically oriented, and emotions are confusing and quick to surface. It is a time of upheaval and
change as youth turn their attention from family to friends, and from
the same to the opposite sex. The naïve sense of security that has previously protected them gives way to self-consciousness and awkwardness as adolescents become more mentally aware. Adolescence is a
time of pulling away, of testing limits, of exploring sexuality, of questioning identity, and of shifting relationships. Physical and intellectual
changes are fast-paced and uncoordinated, and teens struggle to understand who they are becoming. Adolescents need emotional guidance to
negotiate the distance between childhood and young adulthood.

The darker side of adolescence has become a topic of public conversation. Widely distributed magazines, such as *Newsweek* and *Time*,
have focused on the daily activities of adolescents. The teen culture has
been targeted, and its music, language, fashion, and social habits have
been scrutinized. New statistics have been reported on the quantity of
drug and alcohol use, the frequency of sexual activity, the prevalence of
cheating, and the number of suicide attempts. Many of today's adolescents are not given the opportunity to develop healthy relationship
skills. Numerous surveys reveal that a sizeable proportion of students
feel alienated or disconnected from parents, teachers, and classmates.
This alienation is not limited to students out of the mainstream of
school life; even students who are academically successful report isolation (Kantrowitz and Wingert 1999).

The word "safe" carries a range of connotation when used in connection with adolescents and their learning. The school bombings,
bomb threats, and shootings have shattered any lingering mystique of

*Your
Ideas*

schools as institutions impermeable to the ills of society. The concern for the negative influence of the media, for the ease of illicit exchange via the Internet, and for the pressures of conformity inherent in peer groups has raised the issues of teen violence and school safety to new levels of public consciousness. Schools have strengthened security, dress codes have been instated, book bags have been banned, and programs for emotion management have escalated. To go about their business, schools need to be safe places for adolescents to learn.

A flurry of interest has likewise mounted about helping students feel personally "safe," supported, accepted, and valued within the classroom setting (Beamon 1997). Entire issues of *Educational Leadership* have focused on the themes of personalized learning (September 1999), the spirit of education (December-January 1998-99), and creating a climate for learning (September 1996). A high premium has been placed on helping adolescents develop healthy social and emotional behaviors. Teachers have been encouraged to build positive relationships within the classroom, to pay attention to students' feelings and personal needs, to identify signs of alienation, and to help students deal with negative emotions in constructive ways.

Information has also been offered from the field of neuroscience about the brain's activity during aggressive behavior (Sylwester 1999). While emotionally-charged neural responses may lead to quick reactions and self-protective actions, adolescents' brains also have the capacity to override this instinctive response with a more rational one. The emotional overload during adolescence, however, gives this reasoning capacity a real test. To complicate the situation further, because of the range of their prior experiences, some supportive and caring and others not so healthy, adolescents enter puberty and the classroom with different levels of personal and emotional needs. Figure 2.3 indicates a few signs of emotional and social distress that may signal trouble.

Professionals generally agree that adolescents need guidance to cope with the social pressures and personal identity confusion that naturally accompany this transitional time in their lives (Cohen 1999). More effective than expensive school security systems, many educators are looking to classroom teachers to help to promote adolescent social and emotional learning. By creating a safe place for adolescents to learn, teachers can help them deal with the ongoing personal challenges they encounter. In a classroom where the climate is characterized by relationship-building, positive interaction, and trust, adolescents' social and emotional behaviors can be positively directed.

Signs of Emotional and Social Distress

Social Withdrawal

Excessive Feelings of Isolation, Loneliness, or Rejection

Excessive Feelings of Persecution

Uncontrolled Anger

Patterns of Impulsive and Chronic Hitting, Intimidation, and Bullying Behaviors

Low School Interest, Low Academic Performance

Consistent Alcohol or Drug Use

Affiliation with Gangs

Expression of Violence in Writings/Drawings

Serious Threats of Violence

Inappropriate Access, Possession, Use of Firearms

History of Discipline Problems and Violent and Aggressive Behavior

Intolerance for Differences, Prejudices

Figure 2.3

Creating Classroom Connections:
Real and Virtual

To adolescents, the digital world of computers, CD-ROMs, cameras, and video games is as familiar as turning on the television or popping a plate of leftovers into the microwave. They surf through cyberspace as easily as pressing the buttons on a remote control or programming a VCR. They have been called the "net generation," "the N-Geners," and "digital kids" (Tapscott 1999, 7-8). Technology provides a medium for communication, gossip, and instantaneous information exchange as adolescents inquire, explore interests, and develop friendships globally. Used appropriately with adolescents in the classroom, technology can help to foster peer relationships, stimulate critical thinking, facilitate self-expression, build teamwork, and promote self-confidence.

Technology is restructuring curriculum and changing the social, intellectual and personal culture of adolescent learning across the

Your
Ideas

world (Bransford et al. 1999). Tapscott described the Internet as the "ultimate interactive environment." It gives access to "the vast repository of human knowledge, the tools to manage this knowledge, and a growing galaxy of services ranging from sandbox environments for preschoolers to virtual laboratories for medical students studying neural psychiatry" (1999, 9). Interactive software allows the visualization and manipulation of information, and virtual reality has transcended time and distance (Bransford et al. 1999). Students are building local and global communities that include peers, teachers, and practicing professionals. Figure 2.4 shows several classroom examples of the way technology is transforming adolescent learning.

The ACT Model, "Technology and Interdisciplinary Learning," provides an interdisciplinary example appropriate for a team of middle school teachers.

Technology Changes Learning

Middle School Examples

- Desktop teleconferencing has enabled American students to discuss projects with peers in other countries through a NetMeeting. Other project ideas include sharing slides from science experiments; exchanging artifacts from a geological dig; studying the water or air quality by comparing microscopic slides of bacteria, flora, or fauna and discussing remedies for pollution in science; and collecting and tabulating data about local geographical features for a database in social studies or math (McCullen 1999).

- Students used a Web site, electronic field trips, and interactive broadcasts to study the culture and history of the Mississippi River (http://www3.iptv.org/interactive/miss/). Others took virtual journeys through online quests that follow teams of adventurers on trips through foreign countries and collect data about people, culture, wildlife, and social issues (http://www.quest.classroom.com/).

  Other teams compete nationally to build the best educational Web sites (http://www.thinkquest.org) (Fatemi 1999).

- Students in Michigan created hypermedia stacks about books they had read. They incorporated artwork, music, and original raps that addressed relevant social issues (Daniels and Bizar 1998).

High School Examples

- A math class transported data from CD-ROMs and the Internet into spreadsheets, word processors, and graphing calculators to predict population trends, monitor stock activity, and simulate projectile motion (Drier et al. 1999).

- Art classes used computer-graphic-imaging systems to create designs (Page 1999).

- Virtual reality opened a world of manipulation and discovery for other adolescents:

  - A Spanish class visited the ancient Mayan ruins of Chichen Itza;

  - A social studies class traveled back into time to the Battle of 1812;

  - A virtual solar system put students into simulated orbit around the sun;

  - A virtual House of Representatives enabled students to handle a pending bill;

  - A biology class learned cell structure through virtual simulation; and

  - History students toured post-revolutionary thirteen colonies for a virtual constitution (Sykes and Reid 1999).

- An English teacher in New Jersey created a CD-ROM that contains synopses of ancient Greek plays and accompanying artwork from New York's Metropolitan Museum of Art (Fatemi 1999).

- Teams of students stationed at various computer centers in a physics classroom worked on different aspects of concepts such as light refraction (Daniels and Bizar 1998).

- Teams of students created two-minute videos about curriculum topics, including racism, the solar system, and photosynthesis using camcorders and graphics cut from old magazines. They added a script, captions, taped sound effects, and music (Daniels and Bizar 1998).

- An interactive digital network system allowed students and college professors to share projects, such as DNA extraction, water quality testing, nutrition, and weight management, an online science magazine, videoconference writing, a Model United Nations, and town hall meetings (Farley 1999).

Figure 2.4

Technology and Interdisciplinary Learning: Transitions in the Rainforest

Adolescents learn better when they are allowed to work together on relevant tasks and problems. An interdisciplinary team project revolving around a pertinent theme immerses them in a learning experience across content areas. Other benefits include challenging tasks, ongoing feedback on personal progress, a variety of learning products, and a culminating performance assessment. Throughout the experience adolescents are given opportunities to explore ideas, research using technology, and make decisions and choices. Adolescents are highly motivated as they assume increasing responsibility over earning management.

Content Understanding

Theme: Interrelationship

Science: Help students construct knowledge of population dynamics and to analyze practices that affect the use and management of natural resources.

Mathematics: Help students acquire skills for understanding of graphing, probability, and data analysis.

Social Studies: Help students discern the interrelationship among resources, people, plants, and animals.

Language Arts: Help students use language to express individual perspectives and to develop critical thinking skills for persuasive writing.

Technology Skills: Help students use a variety of technologies to access, analyze, apply, and communicate information and learning.

Strategies for Inquiry

A Problem-Based Role Play

Four students will assume the following parts (with props) and present a role play:

- Rainforest Native complains about the land, home, and food disappearing.
- Business Person/Logger says that the company is taking the trees and land to make a living.
- Scientist/Researcher expresses concern for the loss of raw materials for medicines.
- Environmentalist takes the side of the native in protection of the land and its resources.

■ A video documentary about rainforest destruction can be shown, followed by questions, such as What is the major problem? Who are the groups involved in the conflict? What do you currently know about the argument of each?

Guided Interaction

■ The teachers should divide students into the four representative groups with the task of researching this perspective over a two-week period in preparation for a culminating debate.

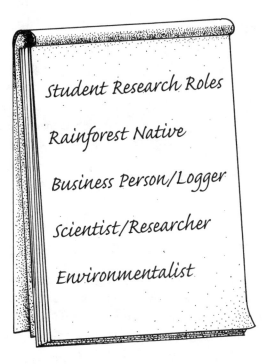

Student Research Roles

Rainforest Native

Business Person/Logger

Scientist/Researcher

Environmentalist

Supporting Learning Experiences Across Classes

■ In science, students can explore the geographical location, climatic conditions, and plant life of rainforests. Comparisons can be compared with areas in the United States and graphs made, and students can respond to the question, Should plant life be preserved in rainforests?

■ In math, students can learn graphing techniques, including histograms, stem, pie and bar graphs, and spreadsheet applications to use with rainforest data. Dates can be

---

Additional Teacher/Student Internet Resources to Facilitate Inquiry

The Smithsonian Center for Tropical Forest Science.
http://www.ctfs.si.edu/

Educational Web Adventures (Amazon Interactive)
http://www.eduweb.com/amazon.html.

Rainforest Information Centre.
http://forests.org/ric/.

Wealth of the Rainforest (Help with Rainforest School Reports).
http://www.rain-tree.com/schoolreports.htm.

Skyrail (Rainforest Research Fund)
http://www.skyrail.com.au/tropeco.htm

Web site research courtesy of S. Howard, S. Simpson, C. Spigle, K. Stack. (2000 May). Elon College, NC.

---

accessed to interpret trends, such as the increase in paved roads or decrease in a kind of vegetation.

■ In social studies, students can participate in guided research according to assigned roles using Internet search engines and Web sites shared by teachers, such as Amazon Interactive (See sidebar on this page.) Their perspectives can be represented by a creative rainforest brochure. They will also learn the techniques for debate.

■ In language arts, students can learn the techniques for persuasive writing. Model essays about other environmental issues, such as marine parks, can be analyzed. Students will ultimately develop a persuasive essay representing a stance on the rainforest issue.

Metacognitive Development and Assessment

■ The culminating project is the debate. A student representative from each group will sit on the debate panel. One or two other students per group could sit on a questioning panel and remaining students and teachers can form an audience. Debate criteria should include logic of presentation, credibility of information, persuasiveness of argument, representation of role, verbal delivery of speech, and involvement in counter-questioning.

Cross-Disciplinary Applications

■ The standard curriculum is a rich source of problems, issues, and themes that connect the content areas. A few that are pertinent to adolescent learning include transitions, identities, interdependence, independence, conflict resolution, justice, social structures, caring and wellness (Stevenson 1998).

A More Responsive Learning Environment

Technology has enhanced the adolescent learning environment in two ways: accessibility to resources and expertise and interactivity within learning communities (Bransford et al. 1999). Instantaneous electronic connection has also enabled teachers, adolescents, and expert practitioners, including scientists and engineers, to form "telecollaborative" communities whose purpose is to build knowledge jointly through inquiry (Bransford et al. 1999, 97). Following the rigorous procedures of professionals in the field, these learning "partners" collaborate about real-world problems. One example is Global Lab, an international community of schools that has formed an electronic network to research large-scale global problems. Students research a local problem, share findings with international peers, and interactively identify common environmental phenomena across the world. These students then collaborate with real scientists to design experiments, conduct peer reviews, and publish findings.

Other examples of technology-supported learning communities are project-based learning, WebQuests, ThinkQuests, and CyberGuides, comparable learning approaches that require students to use technology tools as the medium through which knowledge is built. These experiences promote student inquiry, discussion, teamwork, and an understanding of multidisciplinary concepts (Yoder 1999). Adolescents use traditional and Web-based resources, and usually work toward a common product or project, e.g. a multimedia presentation, a dramatic performance, an interactive Web page, a debate, or a written document. Beyond higher-order knowledge and critical inquiry skills, adolescents also learn to differentiate Web sites that are educationally appropriate.

Some general guidelines for designing Web-based inquiry follow (Yoder 1999, 3–4):

- **Design a compelling inquiry task** that captures adolescents' interest. These situations may ask them to 1) investigate contemporary problems, such as global warming; 2) evaluate historical events; 3) create products; 4) deal with real-life encounters, such as planning a trip, or 5) use their imagination, such as a journey in time or space. A task introduction will help "set the stage."
- **Guide adolescents through the process.** Teachers should facilitate student questioning, assign roles, and help with data collection and time management. Strategies for effective group work or problem solving should be posted.
- **Gather relevant materials and links.** Resources include people, texts, videos, places, and relevant Web sites identified in journals and through search engines.

Your Ideas

- **Evaluate final products.** A rubric, designed by teachers and students, which has a variety of criteria and benchmark levels in each category is the best tool.
- **Conclude.** Adolescents need time to review and reflect on the process of learning and the skills gained through the inquiry.

Some technology resources provide complex problems for adolescents to solve, while others help them identify their own through an extended interactive network with other students and professionals. These are either available to teachers as "stand-alone" software, CD-ROM media, or videodisks, or they can be accessed through Internet locations. Many support the apprenticeship model that links adolescents with expert practitioners who model and guide. All of the resources are interactive tools that challenge adolescents' thinking and enable them to become more self-directive in their learning (see Figure 2.5).

Resources for Technology-Supported Learning Communities
Encouraging Problem Finding

- The GLOBE Program (Global Learning and Observations to Benefit the Environment) consists of student-gathered data about the local environment. Students then create a GLOBE database that they and scientists use for analyses. Students conduct investigations in several earth science areas, including atmosphere, land cover, soils, and hydrology using the instruments and observations designed by real scientists (http://mvspin.gsfc.nasa.gov/SCTB/test/globe.html).

- The Learning Cooperative (American Schools Directory) provides problems in science, literature, social studies, and mathematics (http://www.asd.com/edconn/).

- Learning Through Collaborative Visualization (CoVis) Project are networks of middle and high school students and university researchers as they investigate topics in atmospheric and environmental sciences through visualization software and other inquiry tools (http://www.covis.nwu.edu/).

- The Jason Project (http://www.jasonproject.org/front.html) and GlobaLearn (http://www.GlobaLearn.com/) supplies students with "virtual" global field trips to environments all over the world. The curriculum is designed by real scientists and students can ask questions through two-way audio communication.

- Global Schoolhouse Project (http://www.virtualschool.edu/mon/Academia/GlobalSchoolhouseProject.html) promotes learning clusters of four to six schools to study science topics and exchange ideas.

- Journey North (Annenberg/Center for Public Broadcasting) focuses on problem solving in global and interdependent ecology (http://www.learner.org/jnorth/)

Bringing Challenges To Adolescents

- The Middle School Mathematics Through Application Projects (NMAP) gives students access to innovative software tools to explore concepts in algebra through real-world problems (Institute for Research on Learning).

- The Knowledge Integration Environment (KIE) poses investigative activities and evidence databases generated by scientists, researchers, teachers, and students (http://www.kie.berkeley.edu/KIE.html)

Figure 2.5

The time, energy, personal expertise, and resources needed to use technology effectively in the instruction of adolescents are immense. A recent national survey of teachers' use of digital content by *Education Week* (September, 1999) revealed that a high percentage of teachers are open to the use of technology for instruction, yet they expressed concerns about expense, lack of access to equipment access and training, and problems in getting assistance to align software with specific instructional needs. To assist teachers in their efforts to use technology, some educational magazines supply "Web clips" (Middle Ground) or "Web wonders" (*Educational Leadership*) of useful Internet sites. Teachers can access information, view students' projects and Web pages, read articles, download free software, and order equipment, such as camcorders, digital and document cameras. Figure 2.6 gives a sampling of Internet locations that might be useful as teachers seek to integrate technology into the daily instruction of adolescents. Others are interspersed throughout the book within content-based examples.

The fast-expanding technologies have enabled teachers to create learning environments that better respond to the social, cognitive, and personal needs of adolescents. These environments support sustained exploration and collaborative inquiry about relevant, authentic, and challenging problems. Adolescents assume responsibility, develop confidence, and become competent as they share expertise and construct personal understanding about important knowledge.

Your Ideas

Questioning Instructional Decisions

Teachers who teach with adolescent learning in mind plan differently for instruction and create responsive environments for adolescents' cognitive, social, and emotional development and learning. They model adolescent-centered instruction by doing the following:

- give students more opportunities to solve mathematical word problems;
- allow students to work in pairs or small groups;
- expect students to share their views on current social issues, and debate different sides;
- stress critical thinking daily;
- learn how to conduct Socratic seminars (see chapter 5);
- use technology appropriately;
- spend time talking about what is means to walk in another person's shoes; and
- talk about feelings and emotions, and about positive actions and negative reactions.

Assisting Teachers in Integrating Technology

For General Information, Resources, and Learning Interchange

- TeachersZone.com (http://teacherszone.com/)
- Link2Learn (http://121.org/)
- Technology Education Lab (http://www.techedlab.com/k12.html)
- Service Learning (http://www.ascd.org/); (http://www.doe.state.in.us)
- Young Adult Library Services Association (YALSA) (http://www.ala.org/yalsa/about/vision.html)
- The Apple Learning Interchange (http://www.ali.apple.com/)
- ASCD "Web Wonders" (http://www.ascd.org/readingroom/edlead/9909/mann.html) (http://www.ascd.org/readingroom/edlead/2002/webwonders.html) (http://www.ascd.org/readingroom/edlead/9811/extwebwonders.html)

For Teleconferencing

- CU-SeeMe (http://www.cuseeme.com/software/businessandedu.htm/)
- NetMeeting (http://www.microsoft.com/windows/metmeeting/)
- Global SchoolNet (http://www.gsn.org/cu/)
- Web66 (http://web66.coled.umn.edu/schools.html)

For ThinkQuests

- International Society for Technology in Education (http://www.iste.org/)
- ThinkQuest Internet Challenge (http://www.thinkquest.org/)
- Classroom Connect (http://www.classroomconnect.com/)

Other Inquiry-Based Learning

- Make It Happen: Integrating Inquiry and Technology into the Middle School Curriculum (http://www.edc.org/FSC/MIH/)
- The Exploratorium: Institute for Inquiry (http://www.exploratorium.net/IFI/index.html)
- Smithsonian Education Lesson Plans (http://educate.si.edu.resources/lessons/lessons.html)
- Center for Problem-Based Learning (http://www.imsa.edu/team/cpbl/cpbl.htm)
- The AskERIC Virtual Library, U.S. Department of Education (http://askeric.org/Virtual)
- School World Internet Education (www.schoolworld.asn.au)

For Interactive Learning Labs

- Texas Computer Education Association (TCEA) (www.tcea.org)
- School Tech Expo (www.schooltechexpo.com)
- National Educational Computing Association (www.neccsite.org)

Using Computers Across the Disciplines

- National Council for the Social Studies (http://www.socialstudies.org)
- ArtsEdNet site (http://www.artsednet.getty.edu/); Center for Arts Education (http://www.cae-nyc.org)
- CyberQuests for English-language arts (http://www.buffalostate.edu/~beaverjf/CyberQuests/cyber-HS.html)
- Health-Environmental (http://www.worldbank.org/depweb); (http://www.wri.org);
- Geography (http://magma.nationalgeographic.com/education/maps_geography/index.cfm)
- MATHCOUNTS (http://mathcounts.org/); The Math Forum (http://www.forum.swarthmore.edu/)
- Project-Based Science (http://www.umich.edu/~pbsgroup/)

Figure 2.6

Those teachers realize the importance of active learning experiences that challenge adolescents to discuss ideas, to ask questions, and to work together to solve problems. They use seminars, debates, and case studies and simulations to bring real experiences into the classroom. They understand that knowledge building is not limited to the local setting, and they plan inquiry-based projects that enable students to use technology for communication and information gathering. These teachers are more mindful of adolescents' learning preferences and capabilities as they plan, and they consider content and challenge when they make decisions about instruction. They also pay attention to students' emotional and personal needs.

Your Ideas

Teachers who focus on adolescent learning also consider their relationship with their students in terms of role and responsibility. They realize they need to facilitate understanding rather than to deliver information, to connect with what students know, to demonstrate and model, and to support and give feedback as students work. They recognize that for adolescents to think and learn better, they must interact meaningfully with knowledge, with each other, and with resourceful others. They also realize that for adolescents to become independent they need some degree of choice in how they pursue learning and demonstrate understanding.

Not surprisingly, adolescents agree with what helps and motivates them to think and learn. They want to know the reasons behind historical trends, and they enjoy designing their own art projects. They learn biology better when they work in a school greenhouse, learn math better when they help to construct a shed to house the football team's athletic equipment, and learn music theory better when they write their own compositions. They like to discuss books that relate to their lives, to answer questions that have more than one answer and, as one ninth grader volunteered, they actually prefer assignments that "make you think." They also prefer teachers who understand that "one style won't always work."

Adolescents are similarly forthright about the experiences that they perceive are less supportive of their thinking and learning. They are bored by meaningless facts in a chapter-by-chapter progression. What genuinely frustrates them? Consider a few of their answers:

- I hate to be given busy work.
- I don't like not having anything to do when I get finished with an assignment.
- I wish teachers would vary their teaching methods.
- I get frustrated when I have to figure out something hard like chemistry without help.

Your Ideas

What "turns them off" about teachers? Again, their comments speak:

- I can't respond to teachers who are unfair or "cocky."
- I have a problem with teachers who are inconsistent and set no standards for order or work.
- I don't like it when teachers try too hard to please.
- Sarcastic and insensitive teachers are the worst!

The Chance to Succeed

Adolescents still read aloud passages from Williams' (1999) poignant script of love and betrayal, discuss the causes for major world conflict, balance algebraic equations, and struggle with periodic tables. They face the confusion of identity, the fear of belonging, and the uncertainty of future direction. While the rituals of their daily existence seem perennial and they are perplexed by the changes that have characterized the period of youth for centuries, adolescents today represent a group more diverse, more experienced, more aware, more expectant, and yet more vulnerable than in past decades. Their world is extensive and compelling, and their future promises to be fast-paced and intellectually demanding. Technology has given them new autonomy over learning, broadened their avenues of communication, and heightened their awareness of a sophisticated world.

An environment that supports adolescent thinking and learning should value and understand adolescents. Opportunities should allow students to think together about substantive content and to take responsibility for their achievement and progress. In their future, adolescents must be versed in problem solving and teamwork skills, and they will need to be able to take charge and monitor their own thinking and learning. The quality of their experiences in middle and high school classrooms can provide this preparation. They need to be given the chance.

ACTing
on the Adolescent-Centered Learning Principles Discussed in Chapter 2

Principle	*How I can put it into practice*
❑ Prepare students for the high expectations of the new millennium.	
❑ Broaden avenues of communication among all partners in education.	
❑ Allow for students to share their ideas with others in and beyond classrooms.	
❑ Use technology appropriately as a tool to enhance student thinking and learning.	
❑ Give students a chance to produce high-quality work and see the relevance and purpose in what they are being asked to learn.	

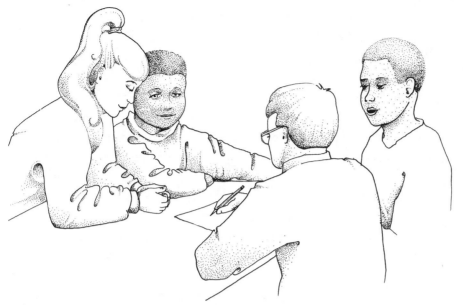

C H A P T E R

3

Structuring an Environment for Learning

The Learning Environment

The differences between the two classrooms were remarkable. In the first, barren walls enclosed rows of students focused on the task of copying a hastily-written geometry problem from an overhead screen in the front of the room. A couple of motivational sports posters were stapled to a side bulletin board. The teacher stood behind the projector, reminding students to work quietly and waiting for a hand to indicate an answer had been found. A female student wearing bright purple gloves asked, "Is that a *one* or a *seven*?" Another put down her pencil and slumped in her desk with the frustrated comment, "I don't even know what a hypotenuse is! I've never done this in my life. I come here every day and have never understood this." A guy in the back called out an answer, and the teacher wrote the solution. Around the room conversations began as another triangle was drawn on the acetate.

In contrast, the second classroom door opened onto a bustle of activity. Pairs of students with rulers, notes, markers, and calculators in hand pored over chart paper. An earlier walk around the school had

yielded ideas for geometry word problems that the students were composing to pass along for classmates to solve. The teacher was spotted, after a couple of minutes, kneeling beside one team whose problem involved finding the area within the triangular support beams of the gym bleachers. Student work peppered the walls. The bulletin board challenged students to post different and creative ways to solve a mystery problem. Over the door frame, an encircled word "EXCUSES," crossed by a diagonal line, clearly specifies the teacher's expectation.

No simple formula exists for structuring an environment that supports adolescent learning, yet several critical elements can be identified. A classroom climate for learning conveys support and respect for students and their ideas. Teacher-student and student-student relationships are interactive, cooperative, positive and caring (Beamon 1997; Danielson 1996). Inquisitiveness is promoted, challenge is apparent, options are given, resources are available, and fair-mindedness is evident. Kohn described an ideal classroom environment as one where teachers work "with students rather than doing things to them" (1996, 54). In these settings, learning is valued and expected, students feel "safe" to take risks with thinking and learning, engagement is high, and all learners, including the teacher, are committed to quality work.

An Adolescent-Centered Perspective

Adolescents have been portrayed as a generation whose experiences, interests, skills, and learning needs have challenged the practices of the traditional classroom. An understanding of how these young people feel, think, interact, and learn is helpful as teachers make instructional decisions that shape the learning environment. The learner-centered concept is an approach that acknowledges the complex interaction of the learner, learning, and the learning environment. McCombs and Whisler defined this perspective as one that combines a focus on the individual learner who varies in heredity, experience, talent, interest, belief system, and capability, with the "best available knowledge about learning" (1997, 9).

Although the personal, intellectual, and social dimensions of an adolescent-centered approach were discussed separately in Chapter 1, it is important to realize that these elements closely interrelate as they affect adolescent learning within the instructional environment (Beamon 1997; Perkins 1992; McCombs and Whisler 1997). Cognitive engagement, for example, involves the personal construction of meaning as adolescents attempt to relate, understand, and reflect upon thinking skill and quality. Learning that is shared helps to strengthen adolescents' knowledge base, promotes feelings of acceptance, and builds self-concept. Learning and thinking that are supported enable adolescents to be intellectual risk-takers as they experiment with ideas, develop tolerance, broaden perspectives, and hone skills for interpersonal relationships.

Your Ideas

An environment based on an adolescent-centered approach does not suggest conformity within classrooms. Some learning experiences do not lend themselves to group activity, technology-enhancement, or student choice. Adolescents do not need to be excused, for example, from reading the classics, learning pertinent formulas, outlining the precipitating events for world conflict, or knowing the specific steps for a lab experiment. Structuring an adolescent-centered learning environment does, however, involve the intentional effort by teachers to help students relate personally, intellectually, and personally in a context that deepens an understanding of content and promotes the skills for higher-level thinking, extended application, and independent learning. The ultimate decision maker is the teacher whose daily challenge is to plan instruction with consideration for the affective, cognitive, and social dimensions of adolescent learning.

Learning Has an Emotional Side

The domain of emotions, often called the affective side of learning, has received much current attention by cognitive psychologists, neuroscientists, and other educators in an attempt to explain the interplay between thinking, feeling, and acting (Gardner 1999; Goleman 1995; Jensen 1998; Sprenger 1999). In some instances, a display of emotions indicates a lack of maturity, though adolescents' emotions are generally understandable reactions. Emotions can interfere with learning or they can contribute to it. Parker Palmer wrote of the role fear plays in students who are "afraid of failing, of not understanding, of being drawn into issues they would rather avoid, of having their ignorance exposed or their prejudices challenged, of looking foolish in front of their peers" (1999, 37). A certain level of cognitive dissonance, however, can catch adolescents' attention and open their minds to new ways of thinking. Terms such as "relaxed alertness" (Caine and Caine 1994) or "unanxious expectation" (Sizer, T. and Sizer, N. 1999) have been used to describe the needed balance between challenge and anxiety in the learning environment.

Studies of the brain's activity have revealed that emotion-related physiological changes take place during the learning process (Caine and Caine 1997; Jensen 1998; Sprenger 1999; Sylwester 1995). As the brain processes information, various chemicals, or neurotransmitters,

*Your
Ideas*

rapidly "fire" information across synapses, or small spaces between nerve cells. During times of mild anxiety, the body's adrenal glands release the substance cortisol, which can provide positive mental alertness. Under more stressful conditions, however, such as when one is humiliated, ridiculed, embarrassed or startled, cortisol is released in high enough levels to interfere with neuron processing.

Under emotionally negative conditions, adolescents are less likely to reason well, to grasp concepts, to understand relationships, or to make full use of the capacities associated with higher-level thinking. When students react to stress, for example, they tend to "pull back" from their optimum performance. In these instances, thinking is limited and learning is impeded. Another related finding from neurological research is that under certain conditions the brain will cause the body to release emotionally "feel-good" chemicals that are beneficial to the thinking and learning process (Jensen 1998; Sprenger 1999). Positive emotions are generated by meaningful gestures of support and acceptance that help to build self-esteem and promote positive self-concept (see Figure 3.1). Positive emotions can also be released through various instructional strategies that encourage social interaction, movement, creativity, and personal choice.

The role of adolescents' emotions cannot be overlooked in the plan for learning. Gardner drew attention to the positive function of emotions: "[If] one wants something to be attended to, mastered and subsequently used, one must be sure to wrap it in a context that engages the emotions"(1999, 76). When adolescents are immersed in a learning situation that stimulates their curiosity and activates their senses, they are more likely to engage emotionally.

Appropriate challenge and intrigue can create an emotional reaction in adolescents that is motivational and healthy. When neural activity is stimulated and feelings are productively engaged, complex learning connections are possible. Gardner observed that students are "more likely to learn, remember, and make subsequent use of those experiences with respect to which they had strong—and one hopes, positive—emotional reactions" (1999, 77). Emotions activated through sarcasm, humiliation, high levels of frustration, unrealistic expectations, embarrassment, minimal feedback, boredom, stifled expression, limited relevance, continual failure, sense of powerlessness, confusion, or lack of resources, however, have a counterproductive effect on adolescent thinking and, consequently, their learning (Jensen 1998; Sprenger 1999).

Merely putting adolescents in touch with challenging learning experiences that stimulate curiosity and engage emotions does not guarantee that they will expend the intellectual energy needed to

Promoting Positive Emotions

Your
Ideas

Actions and Activities

Exercise and movement

Constructive feedback

A smile or affirming pat on the back

A handshake or high five

Music, humor, laughter

Peer interaction

A sense of belonging and relationship

Instructional Strategies

Drama, role play, and debate

Games and simulations

Cooperative learning and team events

Personal expression and journal writing

Celebrations, storytelling, class discussion

Problem-solving, projects, peer editing

Interactive technology

Figure 3.1

accomplish a task in an exemplary manner. The thinking effort adolescents will exert generally depends on certain mental tendencies, or dispositions, closely tied to emotions and feelings (Tishman, Perkins, and Jay 1995). Cultivating an adolescent mindset for good thinking practice is addressed next.

Getting the Right Mindset

Helping adolescents acquire the mindset for higher-level thinking is an ongoing challenge. They have the cognitive ability to take an alternate perspective on an issue, for example, yet they are not generally inclined, or "disposed," to do so unless externally prompted. A social studies teacher might want students to acknowledge the reasoning behind a viewpoint that differs from their own. An issue-laden question, such as, Should the United States government ban immigration? could be offered for discussion. Adolescents' responses will typically reflect

Your Ideas

either the pro side, based on the rationale of economics, job security, and the problems with work visas, or the con side, reflecting America's image to the world as a free and safe haven for the downtrodden. The teacher might then change tactics and ask two students to argue for an opposite perspective. The purpose would not be to make the students change their minds, but rather to understand how another might think in the situation. Another strategy to encourage perspective taking is illustrated in the inquiry-based scenario in the ACT Model, "Encouraging A Mindset for Thinking. "

Encouraging A Mindset for Thinking: Should Immigration Be Banned?

Often adolescents are not "disposed" to tolerate viewpoints that differ from their own. In a situation where they are required to gather and synthesize information that represents varying perspectives, they become more aware of the different experiences that shape personal beliefs. They can also develop the disposition to consider in a fair-minded way the context for others' ideas.

Content Understanding

Help adolescents develop a personal perspective on current social issues based on an awareness of the broader cultural and historical context.

Strategies for Inquiry

An Inquiry-Based Challenge: The rising number of immigrants filing application for permanent citizenship status, the influx of Kosovo refugees, the concerns for illegal immigration, and drug smuggling across the Mexican border have prompted American government officials to schedule a national summit to discuss the problem. Rumor abounds that a ban on immigration might be proposed. You have been asked to serve as teams of youth delegates. Your task is to develop a well-informed presentation that addresses the various perspectives of people involved in the immigration process.

Guided Interaction

- Teams of students can be formed to gather information from a variety of viewpoints. Strategies for data collection could include interviews with local citizens, letters to members of Congress and other government officials, newspaper articles on immigration-related events, and news coverage. Stories that tell of the struggles and perceptions of immigrant families might be located.

- Students should collaborate to develop their researched ideas for the summit simulation. Individual perspectives need to be shared and shaped with choice and creativity allowed. Visuals, technology enhancements, role play or other ways to show findings can be incorporated based on individual learning preferences.

Useful Internet Sites

The Immigration and Naturalization Service
(http://. ins. usdoj. gov/graphics/index. htm)
Provides updates on immigration services and legislative activity

The National Immigration Forum (NIF)
(http://www. immigrationforum. org/).
Gives a pro-diversity perspective

Ellis Island's official Web site
(http://www. ellisisland. org/)
Highlights an immigration museum

ThinkQuest 2000
(http://www. thinkquest. com/) or

The WebQuest Page
(http://www. edweb.sdsu.edu/webquest/webquest.html/).
Includes Web-based inquiry projects on the immigration themes

Metacognitive Development and Assessment

■ Responsibility should be placed on the adolescents to explore resources, acquire and analyze information, and synthesize findings that help shape personal perspectives. At various checkpoints, the teacher should require teams to assess progress and productivity and to revise strategy if needed.

■ The culminating performance-based product will be the summit presentation. Evaluation criteria might include
– Acknowledgement of varying perspectives on issue
– Logical synthesis of data collected
– Valid support for ultimate group perspective
– Appropriate use of enhancements (visuals, handouts, technologies).

■ Individual and peer evaluations can also assess group contribution and collaboration skills. A rubric can be developed (see Figure 3.2).

Group Collaboration Evaluation

Name of Group Member _____

Participated, contributed ideas for team discussions and decisions
1--------------------2--------------------3--------------------4--------------------5

Fulfilled responsibility for "fair share" of work load
1--------------------2--------------------3--------------------4--------------------5

Maintained a positive attitude
1--------------------2--------------------3--------------------4--------------------5

Was a team player
1--------------------2--------------------3--------------------4--------------------5

Figure 3.2

■ Reflection time needs to follow the simulation for the assessment of problem-solving strategies used during the inquiry and their application to other real-world challenges.

Cross Disciplinary Application

■ In science, students could be presented with a problem scenario that proposes a ban on smoking in all public buildings in the United States or globally.

■ In English, students could research the rationale behind a local parental objection to the reading of a particular adolescent novel.

■ In mathematics, adolescents could critique varying methods for solving a problem.

*Your
Ideas*

The willingness to entertain a viewpoint different from one's own is an example of a disposition that supports open-minded thinking (Barell 1995). Robert Ennis (1987), highly regarded for his work in critical thinking and its assessment, emphasized that thinking dispositions are foundational to good thinking ability and need to be cultivated intentionally by teachers (see Figure 3.3). Other educators have combined both disposition and ability when they describe the intellectual traits of good thinkers (Perkins 1992; Tishman, Perkins, and Jay 1995). Dispositions play a critical role in the affective dimension of the learning environment and influence the kind of thinking habits adolescents will potentially develop and use in real life (Paul 1998).

Dispositions for Thinking and Learning

Disposed to:

Question and Pose Problems

Seek Accuracy of Information

Stay Informed and Consider The Broader Situation

Use Credible Sources

Take A Position When Evidence Warrants

Suspend Judgment Of Others' Ideas

Be Fair-Minded, Tolerant and Empathetic

Be Flexible, Careful and Orderly

Be Diligent In The Face Of Ambiguity

Devote Enough Time To Do A Challenging Task Well

Seek and Evaluate Reasons

Sustain Intellectual Curiosity

Be Planful and Strategic

Seek Clarity and Understanding

Be Metacognitive, Reflective, and Self-Evaluative

Figure 3.3

Dispositions are "teachable" over time through favorable and ongoing experiences within the learning environment (Tishman et al. 1995). Structured debate, role play, seminar, and simulation, for example, help adolescents develop tolerance for others' ideas. Inquiry-based problems that stir curiosity can prompt them to wonder, question, probe, and explore information from various angles. Opportunities to reflect upon and evaluate what they have said or prepared can make them increasingly aware of important intellectual standards, such as logical reasoning, clarity, accuracy, and precision.

Your Ideas

Obviously, teachers play an important and active role in the selection of instructional strategies and in the expectations they establish for interactive behavior. When teachers model the dispositions, adolescents are more likely to emulate and internalize them. A few self-assessment questions for teachers to follow are suggested below.

- Do I insist that students listen to each other during discussions?
- Do I have them formulate and ask each other questions?
- Do I have students revise a draft or plan a project?
- Do I ask them to rephrase an answer or elaborate on and substantiate an idea?
- Do I model appropriate mental behaviors, such as explaining aloud the steps in my own reasoning?
- Do I verbally alter my own viewpoint in light of new evidence?
- Do I allow students time to think through ideas or delve deeply into a task?

Key to helping adolescents acquire a mindset for expanded thinking and learning is making them aware of the affective skills they should develop (Barell 1995; Tishman et al. 1995). When teachers ask their students to reflect on what they learned about their own thinking, they provide an opportunity for students to recognize the disadvantage of being narrow-minded. Following the immigration simulation, for example, if students are asked to talk about their feelings, they may see advantage in a broadened perspective. In addition, they may begin to realize the complexity of such issues and approach a new problem with a more flexible frame of mind.

As discussed in earlier chapters, adolescents need assistance in developing and using the metacognitive skills that will help them recognize how and when their thinking improves. Only then can they begin to gauge their own progress and become more effective learners. To acquire the skills for self-regulated thinking and independent learning, adolescents need practice with being in charge. Teachers should share the ownership for learning with their students by giving them more responsibility to make decisions and choices, and more accountability to manage and monitor personal learning direction and effectiveness.

Your Ideas

Making Decisions that Manage Learning

Adolescents did not learn to ride a bike or read or even master their favorite video game by someone else doing the work. Yes, there were training wheels, picture books, and interactive tutorials, and most certainly, parents, teachers, siblings, and friends guided, instructed, and cheered. Ultimately, however, the responsibility for solo performance and the true test of learning rested with the young person. The solo performance for adolescents will be their future use of critical and reasoned thinking, their understanding and tolerance for global diversity, the depth of their knowledge, and their ability to think through challenging and varied circumstances. To be prepared for the future, they need to be held responsible today.

An instructional environment that enables adolescents to assume progressive responsibility for personal thinking and learning is shaped through active involvement and negotiated control. Although at times necessary, if a teacher always determines what and how something is to be learned, or the amount of time needed, or the way learning can be demonstrated, adolescents get no practice in making decisions that manage learning. As frightening as it may seem, teachers need be progressively less directive as they permit, enable, and expect adolescents to be pointedly more directive in the learning process. Learning ownership is built from the sharing of ideas, questions, and strategies early in the learning experience, and continues as adolescents tackle, complete, and reflect back over challenging tasks. It is based on the accumulation of experiences that guide, sometimes nudge, yet consistently and intentionally place responsibility upon the shoulders of adolescents.

Sharing ownership does not mean that teachers take a back seat in the learning environment. On the contrary, whether conducting a lab experiment, working through an algebra problem, composing an essay, or researching a topic, adolescents need guidance as they develop the skills for strategic thinking and good mental management (Tishman et al. 1995). The ACT Model, "Sharing the Ownership of Learning," illustrates shared ownership between a teacher and students.

Sharing the Ownership for Learning

Shared ownership among teachers and students enables adolescents to assume responsibility over their learning progressively. Teacher guidance, more apparent early in the interaction, decreases as adolescent self-management increases. Through this process, student metacognitive growth is promoted. The following steps can be applied to any project-based inquiry or academic challenge.

Content Understanding

- ■ The teacher and students set goals for various stages of the learning process.

> ### Planning Goals
>
> What is the problem to be investigated?
>
> Where and when should data be collected?
>
> How should data be analyzed?
>
> Where should progress be checked?
>
> What are the steps needed to complete the final product or performance?

- ■ The teacher and students discuss criteria and standards as guidelines for and evaluation of final product. Expectations are communicated for individual contribution and group collaboration.

Strategies for Inquiry

■ The teacher helps students identify the steps for strategic planning.

Planning Strategy

What questions must be
  answered?

Which contacts should be
  arranged?

What format should be used for
  data display?

What resources will be needed?

■ The teacher helps students identify the various people affected by or involved in the issue at hand.

■ Under the teacher's guidance, the class identifies any underlying procedures they need to understand. Teams of students begin to plan research strategies for data collection, such as Web searches, online visits to newspaper archives, or interviews.

Guided Interaction

■ During the task, the teacher reminds students to stay mentally open to new information that might strengthen a final product.

■ The teacher gives feedback to student responses, pointers on their research questions, assistance with avenues for information, and guidance as they interpret findings, shape conclusions, and prepare for the final product.

■ The teacher reminds students of their goals and asks them to check their work periodically.

Metacognitive Development and Assessment

■ When a simulation or experience is over, the teacher provides a pocket of time for students to reflect on the quality of the end product with regard to set standards, and of the effectiveness of the strategies used during the entire process.

A Time for Reflection

At what stages were your ideas validated?

When was your reasoning logical?

In what ways was your analysis thorough?

How did you know your resolutions were sound?

Cross-Disciplinary Applications

■ In English teachers and students monitor the planning and evaluation of a research project on an author in a specific time period. A presentation of the author's style and historical context as the end product.

■ A science/mathematics teacher team and students might collaborate to design a nature trail and navigation guide based on the metrics system.

*Your
Ideas*

Adolescents have the metacognitive capacity to evaluate their thinking quality, yet they may lack a mental model or clear sense of what good thinking looks and sounds like (Perkins 1992). Adolescents are often unlikely to assess the effectiveness of a way of thinking, or how to adapt an approach to a different situation unless the teacher helps them make this connection. Sharing ownership requires teachers to interact with adolescents continually and meaningfully over the course of the learning experience.

The similarity of a learning situation to the real-world context influences how well adolescents retain the content knowledge and use the skills in related experiences. If adolescents associate the knowledge and skills only with a particular context, they are not likely to transfer learning to another situation (Bransford et al. 1999).

Is the Context Real Enough?

Two math classes were sharply contrasted at the beginning of this chapter. In the first, students were copying a teacher-formulated problem from the overhead and using a specific formula to find the appropriate answer. In the second, pairs of math students were designing geometry problems based on real surroundings for peers to solve. In which instance are the students likely to remember what they have learned? Which students will be more likely to notice evidence of mathematics in the real world?

The answer is obvious. In the second example, adolescents are challenged to apply what they know about a geometric concept through an original problem. They make personal decisions about relevant problem topics, and they share their ideas. When the context of the learning experience is meaningful and responsive to adolescents as learners, they are more apt to connect, remember, and apply it to other areas of learning.

Most teachers can recall a time when students, after dutifully memorizing formulas and facts, were confounded by a changed context, such as a word problem or a different application situation. The likelihood is slim that students will apply the content and thinking appropriately in another context, particularly if the experience lacked relevance or the teacher does not help establish a connection (Perkins 1992). Adolescents who discuss the events of the Holocaust, for example, may not readily see any parallel to the genocide in modern-day Albania. Those who learn the Pythagorean theorem may not recognize its applicability in drafting class or its necessity in the calculation of the length of a slanted roof. Likewise, students may attribute a perfect foul shot to the skill of a ball player without any thought of the principles of physics that make it possible.

Learning is believed to be influenced by the surrounding context, or situation (Alexander and Murphy 1998). Cognitive psychologists use the term "situated cognition" to refer to the phenomenon that knowledge and skills may be "contextualized" within a particular learning experience (Greeno 1998; Resnick 1991). The context for adolescent learning includes the content of the lesson, the instructional activity, and the opportunities for interaction and involvement. One might consider the following illustrations:

Students who . . .

- enact a model United Nations better understand the real-world concepts of negotiation and interdependence.
- run a class business gain relevant knowledge of the principles of consumer mathematics.
- simulate a town meeting to discuss the impact of a proposed thoroughfare near the school begin to take civic responsibility more seriously.
- adopt a local creek, monitor variables, such as odor, clarity, temperature, and velocity, and observe the activity of plants and "critters," gain hands-on knowledge of natural habitat and ecological harmony.
- design multimedia book reports for use in the school media center gain a "working" understanding of the elements of style, theme, plot, and characterization.

When the context is "real enough," adolescents are more likely to make pertinent connections with other areas of learning or with comparable situations in everyday life. A context that is shaped chiefly by information intake, little application, and minimal intellectual exchange, however, will limit adolescent understanding and the potential connection with other experiences.

A challenge lies, nevertheless, in shaping a learning context that is "real enough" for the variety of adolescents in a world of change in the midst of a knowledge explosion. If learning is considered to be context-connected, is it also possible for a realistic instructional situation to be so specific that it actually limits the possibility for transfer? Or, if adolescents are immersed in authentic learning experiences, is there any assurance that they will know when the application to another situation is appropriate or judge when a particular approach is working?

Fogarty and Bellanca (1995a), who urge teachers to consider the skills students will need in the future, believe students should learn how

Your Ideas

to relate, how to learn, and how to choose. A "real" learning context for adolescents, then, is one in which they develop the skills for collaboration and personal connection, where they learn about their own learning and how to manage it, and where they practice the skills for knowledge acquisition, analysis, and evaluation.

Cooperative learning, inquiry, problem-solving teams, networking within the broader community through interactive technologies, mentoring, and apprenticeship programs are appropriate contexts for adolescent learning. In such contexts, students are expected to conduct and interpret research, to grapple with moral and ethical issues, to practice reasoning and decision-making, and to hone their skills for reflection and evaluation.

The learning context teaches through its structure and opportunity for interaction (Sizer, T. and Sizer, N. 1999). An effective learning context involves the active and dynamic sharing of ideas, knowledge, and strategy, and it is shaped by caring and support. While there is no guarantee that adolescents will transfer their learning and skills into new, related or real-life situations, scholars such as Bransford et al. (1999) and Perkins (1992) agree that the teachers' role as decision maker is key. Prime consideration lies in helping adolescents develop the capacity for flexible problem solving and a metacognitive awareness of the thinking strategies they might use in other learning situations.

Creating a Community of Learners

Adolescent learning can take place in pairs or small clusters, through individual or group activity, within the classroom setting or through extended connections. Students in chemistry can be partnered for a lab experiment, for example, or sculpting stations positioned around an art room. Students in science class may be "dialoguing" online with youth in Scandinavia about local efforts to regulate acid rain destruction or learning about digital imaging with undergraduates at a local college. A community of learners is one that is engaged in intentional and meaningful activity in a climate of support, acceptance, and high expectancy.

The scenario in the ACT Model, "Art Has a Story to Tell," is an example of the way a community of learners might be created. The teacher is trying to help students understand that they can observe much about an artist or culture through critical observation. Assumptions, though useful to guide thinking, should be tested for accuracy through information acquisition and analysis. The teacher has structured the learning experience to enable the adolescents to share ideas within pairs, within the larger group, and within selected teams.

These students must further interact with pertinent information sources in order to check the accuracy of their assumptions. To complete the task, they will collaboratively draw conclusions from their findings and return to the larger discussion.

Your Ideas

Art Has a Story to Tell

When adolescents are allowed to share ideas and work together on a task they perceive as meaningful, they feel a sense of collective purpose and individual contribution. Under a teacher's careful planning and facilitation, a community of learners begins to form. This learning community should also extend beyond the classroom to include others who can provide pertinent resources, skills, knowledge, and expertise.

Content Understanding

To help adolescents use critical analysis skills in the visual arts to gain an understanding of artists' style within an historical and cultural context.

Strategies for Inquiry: A Challenge Question

What does a piece of art tell us about a person, a period of time, or a culture?

■ Students should jot down personal thoughts to the question, pair to exchange ideas, and share aloud with the class. These might be recorded on the board under "What We Know." Responses might vary from references to artists' eccentric personalities to a reflection of nature.

■ Teachers can exhibit a piece of work, such as an oil-painted Egyptian papyrus, and inquire further: What assumption might you make about this work of art? Student responses might include the use of vivid colors, the importance of religious ceremony, and the symbolism of plants and animals.

Guided Interaction

■ Several art objects and prints can be placed at various locations around the room. These might include a reproduction of a Degas dancer placed on a small table, wall prints by artists, such as Monet, Kandinsky, Klimt, and Picasso, a clay replica of a Xian soldier, a hand painted Chinese medicine bottle, or a watercolor by a Kenyan youth. Envelopes can be placed beside each with enclosed identifying information. Students should be divided into investigative teams of four or five and presented with the following instructions:

Instructions for Investigative Teams

1. Visit three stations and discuss your assumptions about the art piece.
2. Record group observations.
3. Open envelopes to confirm the artist's name, period, or culture.
4. Use these clues to locate information on the Internet about the art piece or form.
5. Test the accuracy of your observations. Be ready to share your learning.

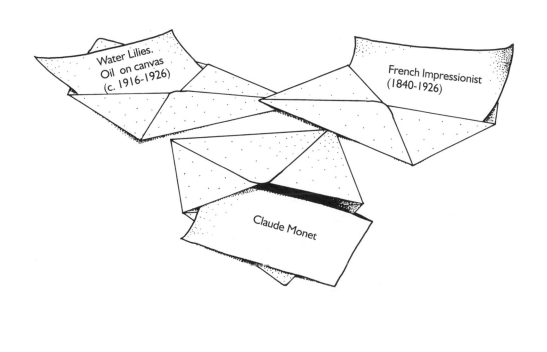

Water Lilies.
Oil on canvas
(c. 1916-1926)

French Impressionist
(1840-1926)

Claude Monet

Metacognitive Development

■ Following the group investigation, teachers should return to the original question. Students' new ideas should be recorded on the board under the category of "What We've Learned," and they should be asked to compare the two sets of responses.

■ Adolescents should be asked to formulate conclusions about the advantages and disadvantages of making assumptions. They should be asked to think of other times when assumption testing would be useful. They can also respond individually in their art reflection journals on what they had learned about art's story and assumption testing.

Cross Disciplinary Applications

■ In social studies, adolescents might examine a collection of editorial cartoons on a topic, such as nuclear disarmament or gun control, and assess the various artists' political perspectives on the issues.

■ In science, students could speculate and determine with rationale which other planet in the solar system could support life comparable to Earth.

■ In mathematics, students could work together to plan the best location for a "chunnel" between the Chinese mainland and the island of Hong Kong.

A community of learners is created when adolescents and teachers share ideas as they work together to expand what they know and improve how they think. A sense of relationship is built among the students through purposeful involvement in a high-level task. The situation itself is realistic and allows the use of resources beyond the immediate classroom to gather information and test personal ideas. Adolescents have an opportunity to inquire actively, to examine instances when their thinking might be shortsighted or superficial, and to reflect upon the importance of well-informed conclusions. The climate is one of sharing, support, and respect.

Your Ideas

The concept of a learning community also involves purposeful interaction among students and meaningful interplay between them and others who are more skilled or knowledgeable. The Russian psychologist Lev Vygotsky (1962) recognized that meaningful exchange within a social context helps students to sharpen skills for higher-order thinking. He proposed that cognitive development is facilitated and enhanced through students' interactions with more advanced or capable others. Vygotsky's observations affirm the teacher's ongoing task to model, probe, and guide student thinking and learning. The term scaffolding has been used to describe the various techniques teachers can use to assist students' efforts to master new content or manner of thinking (Ormond 1999).

Vygotsky's ideas further justify the need for adolescents to interact with others in the extended community. These connections enrich adolescent learning by adding pertinent information based on real-life experiences and expertise. Outside "experts" can also provide helpful feedback to finished products or final performances. When teachers and significant others help adolescents think through the steps of a task, pose questions, articulate their reasoning, and reflect upon how improvements could be made, critical metacognitive skills are fostered. This relationship, frequently referred to as cognitive apprenticeship, is more explicitly illustrated in chapter 4.

Teachers in any discipline can plan learning experiences that build communities of learners. Cooperative activities, such as paired thinking in the art class, or team problem building, as in the math example, allow adolescents to interact within the social milieu of the classroom. Group investigation and inquiry tasks promote peer collaboration and extend the social context to experts beyond. Interaction can be symbolic, as adolescents reflect and write about their thoughts in journals, search for helpful information on the Web, and use virtual reality, or interaction can be with real people. These opportunities put adolescents in contact with the valuable resources in the learning environment and help promote the belief that learning is indeed a socially shared phenomenon.

*Your
Ideas*

Using Assessment to a Cognitive Advantage

How does one assess adolescent understanding? Various teachers have shared their ideas:

- I place large maps of the world in the school commons and assign students problems that require them to use longitude and latitude knowledge. I want to find out if they understand geographic location.
- My students simulate a wax museum of important historical figures. Each "model" is required to represent five characteristics of the person. They also write a monologue and design a banner that displays various genre of writing that figure would have produced.
- To show understanding of weight and equations, my class builds a math bridge.
- To demonstrate their understanding of a certain time period in 20th century history, my students develop a timeline, write interview questions about the period, visit an assisted living facility to interview people who lived during that time, and share the information with classmates.
- To show they understand the concept of survival, my students make backpacks for survival in a chosen biome.
- To assess their understanding of literary perspective, I ask my students to write letters from the viewpoint of a character to someone in real life.
- To show understanding of geometry concepts, my class describes in writing how to derive a formula for the number of blocks in a pyramid.
- My class designs a carnival game as a culminating project for a unit on probability.

Other ideas include the assessment of environmental concepts through a travel brochure, of the justice system by a trial simulation, of the scientific process through a laboratory investigation, and of concepts in economics through the design of a campaign to attract business into an area. Adolescents build models of castles, role play literary events, create Web pages, perform newscasts, write historical poems, make drawings of scientific concepts, structure debates, and prepare book talks. They create postcards, magazines, newspapers, joke books, dances, computer maps, children's books, and multimedia presentations.

These assessment strategies share a few basic ideas. First, these teachers recognize that adolescents have different intellectual strengths, learn differently, and show their understanding in different ways. The examples support a variety of learning preferences. Secondly, these teachers apparently believe that adolescents are motivated when they are actively involved in something that makes sense to them. The strategies call for a demonstration of understanding within the context of the learning experience. Leading proponents of authentic assessment, including Wiggins and McTigue (1998), Gardner (1991, 1999), Perkins (1991, 1992), and Stiggins (1994), might refer to these assessment examples as "contextualized performances of understanding. " Rather than tests of facts that students have memorized, these measures assess understanding through meaningful application in a context closely connected to the learning experience itself. Adolescents would need to know the content well in order to perform the task.

Perkins (1991, 76) defined "understanding performance" as the evidence that makes apparent a student's insight into knowledge:

> Suppose, for example, that a learner can explain the law of supply and demand in his or her own words (not just recite a canned definition), can exemplify its use in fresh contexts, can make analogies to novel situations (let us say to grades in school rather than the cost of goods), can generalize the law, recognizing other laws or principles with the same form, and so on. We probably would be pretty impressed by such a learner's insight into the law of supply and demand.

According to Wiggins and McTigue (1998), six facets indicate true understanding of knowledge (see Figure 3.4). They also observed that "[u]nderstanding is always a matter of degree, typically furthered by questions and lines of inquiry that arise from reflection, discussion, and use of ideas . . . " (1998, 45). For assessment to be used to adolescents' cognitive advantage, it should be an ongoing and integral part of learning experiences. When it is connected closely with instruction, it draws adolescents' attention to what they know, believe, and understand. It also provides an opportunity to give feedback to adolescents as they progress. The ultimate goal of assessment is to help adolescents acknowledge and internalize the standards and cognitive skills for more sophisticated understanding, and become more self-directive in their learning.

A critical factor in making assessment work to adolescents' cognitive advantage lies in establishing a shared mindset for progress and continual personal improvement. The classroom conversation should focus less on what will be on the test and more on how a student might write more logically, contribute more fully to a discussion, or write more coherently (Wiggins 1997). The teacher's role is to guide and facilitate, to give continual feedback, to provide multiple opportunities for learning, and to help students acquire the skills for self-evaluation.

Your Ideas

When Adolescents Really Understand

They Should Be Able To:

1. **Explain it.** How can you explain the impact of this war on the country's economy? What accounts for this conclusion? What is implied in this action?

2. **Interpret it.** What makes sense about this play's ending? How does this style of writing reflect the political climate of the period? How does this historical event illustrate a pattern in human behavior?

3. **Apply it.** How can this knowledge of statistics be used in a different situation? In what real-world context is this economic principle applicable?

4. **Take a perspective on it.** What are the two sides of this political debate? From whose viewpoint is this article written? What are the strengths and weaknesses of this rationale?

5. **Show empathy about it.** How would you feel if you were in an immigrant's shoes? How would these changes impact the way of life for this culture? How are these decisions detrimental to these peoples' well-being?

6. **Gain self-knowledge through it.** What prejudices am I recognizing in myself? How might I formulate questions better? Where was my thinking faulty? How can I use these suggestions constructively?

Figure 3.4

Teachers should also be clear about the standards toward which they hope adolescents will strive and help students understand expectations for exemplary performance. The ACT Model, "Using Assessment to Promote Learning Management," illustrates an assessment strategy designed to promote purposeful collaboration and learner autonomy.

Using Assessment to Promote Learning Management: Making Literary Style Your Own

Assessment can be used to help adolescents develop skills to manage their own learning. This application is a culminating assessment that can serve as a final exam. Previous and more structured and teacher-guided activities, such as group presentations on other readings, would help establish expectations for small group interaction and interpretive analysis. This experience assesses understanding of specific literary elements, such as theme, style, symbolism, and characterization, and allows for individual choice and creative expression.

Content Understanding

To enable adolescents to communicate an understanding of literary elements in fiction and demonstrate skills for interpretive analysis.

Strategies for Inquiry: An Inquiry Group Task

Students are presented with the following instructions:

> Read and discuss your group's book according to theme, symbolism, characterization, and style. Plan a creative presentation that conveys your group's interpretation of these literary elements.

Guided Interaction

- Students should be divided into small groups of four or five based on their common preference of a book from a recommended reading list.
- Specific days need to be designated as "discussion days" and students should be helped to develop a schedule for reading and discussion.
- In preparation for the presentations, teachers should encourage adolescents to be creative, to integrate the arts, such as dance, movement, and music, or to use technology enhancement.

Metacognitive Development and Assessment

■ During discussions and planning sessions, teachers can monitor and offer needed assistance but should not become an integral part of the discussion or planning.

■ Assessment should be in the form of a group grade for the project and individual scores for students' collaborative skills within groups. Students should be involved in the formulation of evaluative criteria and should help determine descriptors for various levels of the rubrics.

Rubric Descriptors for Group Project

Criteria	Outstanding	Meets Expectations	Needs Improvement
Literary Elements (theme, symbolism, characterization, style)	Insightful Interpretation	Adequate, Correct Interpretation	Misconceptions Noted in Analysis
Use of Enhancements (music, art, dance, technology).	Creative, Appropriate	Supporting Use	Minimal Use

Criteria for social skills assessment can include
• participation
• contribution of new ideas
• prompting others to question.

Figure 3.5

■ Teachers should provide a "debriefing" time following presentations when adolescents can think back over the process of the book analysis and reflect on their group's decision-making and interpretive strategies.

Adapted from material provided by D. Scott of Burlington, S.C.

Adolescents need a good representation, or "mental model," of what they should try to emulate for outstanding performance on any task (Perkins 1992). For assessment to work "cognitively," they must also learn to recognize a "work in progress." They need to have a sense of certain "benchmarks" along the continuum that can guide and help them to gauge personal progress (Gardner 1991). A good rubric, collaboratively created based on tangible examples of real work, becomes an important cognitive tool. The "tips" in Figure 3.6 can help teachers design rubrics that enhance adolescent cognitive development (Simpkins 1999).

Your Ideas

Tips for Good Rubric Design

1. Select criteria that are both teachable and measurable. A debate, for example, might include "presentation of argument," information sources," "verbal delivery of speech," or "involvement in counter-questioning. " A multimedia project might be assessed according to screen design, content knowledge, originality, and mechanics.

2. Choose descriptors that communicate clearly what the criteria levels mean. Quality words should be convey what is "outstanding," or "successful," or "needs improvement" on a particular assignment or performance. Descriptors such as "authentic," "detailed," "varied," and "well-documented," for example, might denote strong evidence, while unacceptable work might be "undocumented" and "superficial. "

3. Limit the number of criteria to be assessed and the number of levels for each. Five criteria and four levels are manageable numbers for teachers and adolescents.

4. Involve students in the design or adaptation. This suggestion is critical if adolescents are to become aware of the benchmarks for personal progress.

5. Don't always reinvent the wheel. Teachers are encouraged to develop rubric formats that can be modified and adapted for similar tasks. Numerous rubric models are also available. For example, The National Center for Research on Evaluation, Standards, and Student Testing (CRESST) has rubrics available online at: http://www.crest96. cse.ucla.edu/crest.htm

Figure 3.6

Assessment, used strategically, can help adolescents develop the skills for self-directed learning. As Wiggins aptly expressed, "When they understand what they are expected to learn, students can play a major role in setting immediate and long-range goals and assessing their own progress, much as they track their scores on computer games and their performance in athletics" (1999, 45). As adolescents become more adept at self-assessment, they will be better prepared for success in the world beyond the classroom. Other assessment strate-

gies that promote adolescent autonomy include student-led or student-involved conferences, digital and product portfolios, senior projects, and other forms of publications, and other exhibitions, performances or fairs that involve outside experts, business leaders, college professors, and other community members who share expertise.

The Classes They'll Talk About

The writing prompt on the chalkboard explained the somber activity of the ninth grade classroom: How does it make you feel when you hear that someone close to your age has died? Does it change your reaction when the death is the result of something sudden? Students of varying size and dress pored over journals, their feelings flowing into words on paper. One student sat partially secluded by a screen, a lop-eared stuffed animal clutched under one arm. As was later apparent, this option was open to any student who was having a particularly difficult day, no questions asked. Motivational posters promote individual responsibility, respect for others, and emotional management. On this day an element of reality permeated the group: a car accident earlier in the week had killed two seventeen-year-old schoolmates. Real-life experience permeated the walls of the classroom and adolescent minds were perplexed.

Adolescents understandably talk positively about the classes they enjoy and negatively about the experiences that seem meaningless. They can recognize when an assignment is purposeful, why something is not working, or what "turns them on" to learning. Structuring an environment where adolescents feel personally motivated and emotionally engaged, where they are intellectually charged to think deeply about and understand content more fully, and where they can interact collaboratively and realistically is an ongoing challenge for teachers in any content area.

Nearly two decades ago, Harvard educator Sara Lawrence Lightfoot (1983), wrote the award-winning book, *The Good High School.* She used the term "intellectual play" to describe classrooms where adolescents' personal, cognitive, and social learning needs were met. Intellectual play is possible in classrooms where the atmosphere is comfortable and nonthreatening, and where teachers' expectations are appropriate and apparent to students. It is likely to occur in a creative, challenging, and interactive environment where student relationships are promoted, their ideas are valued, and knowledge is built collaboratively. It is unlikely to occur, however, in a highly competitive setting where teachers are controlling and students are passive and acquiescent. Teachers can thus create environments conducive to adolescent learning by the expectations they set and by the way they strategically interact with students.

Your Ideas

Perkins (1992) used the phrase "culture of thoughtfulness" to describe a learning setting where teachers model, expect, make time for thought, and push for deeper understanding. In this environment, teachers encourage students to explain their thinking, to use their imaginations, and to articulate their ideas. They insist that students pay attention to their thinking and how it is expressed. They provide the opportunity for students to use extended resources, to make personal choices, to assume responsibility, to reflect on their thinking and learning, and to practice important interpersonal and cognitive skills. They also expect adolescents to expend the intellectual energy needed to do an assignment well, and they challenge them to acquire a deeper understanding of content and of their own thinking capabilities.

In these classrooms, adolescents follow the lead by raising questions, by listening, and by learning to reason thoughtfully and logically. Under the expectation to reconsider, to re-examine, to clarify, to elaborate, or to delve deeply, they develop higher standards for their own thinking, reasoning, and learning. They practice valuable skills that help them interact meaningfully with people and information beyond the specific learning experience. In a climate of acceptance and tolerance, adolescents become more flexible, empathetic, and knowledgeable. These are the classes adolescents talk about, and these are the ones they will continue to appreciate.

Reflection and Interchange

Parker Palmer (1998, 74–77) used the words "creative tension" to describe the atmosphere of a classroom when skillful teachers purposefully shape a space for learning. In paradoxical language, he noted the need for both openness and boundary, as students speak and explore, teachers guide, and resources compel. He indicated that the space for learning should be both hospitable and "charged," a "safe" place for ideas, yet expectant of a deep level of exchange. This space should encourage students to voice their individuality, yet learn under the teacher's expectation and to be open to the voice of the group. Within this space for learning, the teacher should connect the inner stories of the student with the bigger stories of the discipline as students seek greater understanding. The space should also allow time for inner reflection and outward interchange as resources are shared and personal understanding is achieved.

Your
Ideas

A space for adolescent learning requires this same kind of preparation. Their emotions must be intentionally engaged, their intellects meaningfully challenged, and their relationships built within a respectful, interactive, and authentic context. Conversely, under negatively charged conditions or in the absence of relevance, stimulation, interchange, or resource, adolescent learning and thinking are physiologically, psychologically, and physically short-changed. A skilled and caring teacher acknowledges and accommodates the interacting affective, cognitive, and social factors that affect adolescent learning and makes instructional decisions accordingly. In this space, adolescents can acquire a mindset for good thinking practice, become responsible and self-motivated learners, and develop the intellectual and personal skills needed to manage in a complex society. This space is a safe one for adolescent learning.

ACTing
on the Adolescent-Centered Learning
Principles Discussed in Chapter 3

Principle	*How I can put it into practice*
❏ Structure a learning environment that is conducive to adolescent thinking and learning by being responsive to students' personal, intellectual, and social needs.	
❏ Build relationships within a respectful, interactive, and authentic context.	
❏ Motivate adolescents to take more responsibility within the learning experience.	
❏ Intentionally engage emotions.	
❏ Challenge adolescent minds with an interactive and personally affirming instructional environment that is supportive and nonthreatening.	
❏ Hold students accountable for good work and continual improvement.	
❏ Demonstrate a caring attitude by listening to student ideas and providing a safe place for them to voice their individuality.	
❏ Help adolescents examine their assumptions.	
❏ Present realistic and worthwhile tasks.	

4

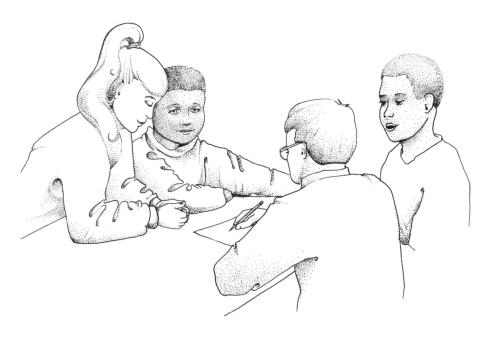

Teaching with Learning in Mind

Stand Up for Adolescent Learning

During the Fourth Annual Teaching for Intelligence in San Francisco (1999), Renate Caine, noted author and proponent for brain-based education, surprised the audience of educators with this statement: "It's time to stand up for learning." Since learning has long been the "business" of schools, Caine's challenge seemed unnecessary. The growing "disconnect" between how students learn and how they are taught, however, is a concern Caine shares with many other professionals in the field (Gardner 1991; Darling-Hammond 1997; Perkins 1992; Sizer 1992, 1996). This disconnect becomes evident in classrooms where the curriculum and instructional practices are incongruent with the personal, intellectual, and social needs of the adolescent learner.

Teachers who stand up for adolescent learning create classroom environments that are "cognitively busy places" (Danielson 1996, 81). They place high value on students' ideas and abilities, the content to be learned, intellectual interaction, and quality in accomplishment. In these classrooms, adolescents know that their thinking will be thought-

Your Ideas

fully received and appropriately challenged by someone who cares about them as individuals, as learners, and as thinkers. They are also motivated by a pervasive standard for personal improvement and progress, and they work hard to do well. This chapter focuses on instructional practices that emphasize meaningful knowledge construction, mastery of content, thinking development, and social interaction.

At Last, Some Theoretical Agreement

Lauren Resnick (1999b), a distinguished cognitive scholar at the University of Pittsburgh, has called for a new direction in teaching that promotes thoughtful learning and strategic thinking development. Her ideas place high premium on purposeful knowledge building and teaching for understanding. The goal of learning, according to Resnick, is to help students become responsible managers of their own cognition. She has proposed that knowledge is not a collection of facts but rather the meaningful interpretation of ideas. Knowledge is also contextualized, or related to the situation where it is learned. She described learning as the socially-shared construction of knowledge, though thinking is highly dependent on the mental manipulation of the individual learner.

Educators committed to the study of learning and the craftsmanship of teaching have begun to share similar ideas about adolescent learning. Four strands can be identified as common across the cognitive science, socio-cognitive, and brain-based learning literature. These tenets are listed below and described in greater detail in the following sections. Figure 4.1 depicts their interrelationship in the classroom environment.

Adolescent learning . . .

- involves active mental processing by the learner;
- is enhanced by purposeful interaction;
- necessitates thinking about knowledge in meaningful ways; and
- thrives in a context of social-emotional support.

Learning Is Active

Adolescents do not merely "absorb" information to reproduce it, although that is sometimes expected in schools (Shuell 1993). They actively construct personal meaning based on how they relate to or make sense of what they are trying to learn or understand. Current studies of the brain's activity during learning show that the mind constantly attempts to "chunk" together and organize pieces of new information with what is already familiar in the individual's knowledge base or personal experience (Caine and Caine 1997; Jensen 1998). The cog-

A Convergence of Theory About Learning

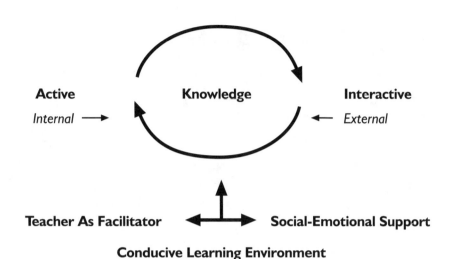

Figure 4.1

nitive structures, or schemas, that form a network of unrelated information can be accessed through memory and future associations. The learning process is highly individual and internal, and it depends heavily on the knowledge, experiences, and other schemata in place at the time (Danielson 1996). Teachers may try hard to impose knowledge upon adolescents, yet the extent students internalize and remember it is based on how well they are able to connect the new learning with what they know, believe, and feel. The ACT Model, "Learning as Active Meaning Making," provides an example.

Process Algebra —

Learning As Active Meaning Making: Can You Think Like a Poet?

Adolescents at times have a perception that poetry is boring and difficult to understand. Teachers have to work strategically to help them relate poetical imagery and abstract ideas to personal experiences. One instructional strategy is to enable them to think like poets. Here, T. S. Eliot is the poet being studied.

Content Understanding

To help adolescents learn to explicate metaphorical imagery in poetry.

Strategies for Inquiry

■ As a preliminary exercise, students could write a personal interpretation of abstract images. These concepts might include peace, silence, loneliness, relationship, betrayal, or others that seem relevant to their lives.

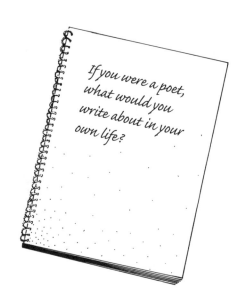

If you were a poet, what would you write about in your own life?

■ After a few students share aloud, a teacher can ask if the images they created with words sound poetic. Teachers can explain that poetry is written about something that is important to someone. Poems have a meaning that is personally relevant to the poet. Each word of a poem is carefully chosen by the poet to convey this meaning.

■ Students also need to have prior knowledge of the political and social nature of early 20th century America. The novels of F. Scott Fitzgerald, Ernest Hemingway, or John Steinbeck, for example, provide rich fictional accounts of this historical period.

The Inquiry Mindset

Imagine yourself as a poet living during a time when you felt personal frustration about what was happening in your native country and in his own life. Imagine you are so frustrated with what you perceive as a society devoid of values or morality that you decide to renounce your citizenship and move to another country.

Guided Interaction

- The teacher might read aloud the first stanza of Eliot's "The Hollow Men" and ask students to try and visualize the figurative images conveyed. Questions might include
  - How can a person's head seem like it's full of straw?
  - Can there be shape without form? Or shade without color?
  - When can a gesture be without motion?
  - Can someone be alive but still feel dead? When?
- Students can be told to visualize a cartoon box out of which a character cannot escape or someone trapped in jail looking out on life.
- An explanation of the term oxymoron as a contradiction of words can be constructed. Other examples might include deafening silence or blind vision.
  - Can a person be blind to life? How?
  - How do Eliot's words make you feel? Have you ever felt "hollow"?
- The remaining stanzas might be read aloud by various students. Groups of students can be assigned specific verses to explicate, and interpretations can be shared and discussed.
- Students might read about another early 20th century poet and analyze at least one poem in terms of this poet's personal, political, or religious beliefs or cultural context. These can be discussed and contrasted.

Metacognitive Development and Assessment

- Students can work individually or in pairs to construct a short poem (free verse is acceptable) that conveys a relevant message, personal feeling, or concern they have as adolescents. A software program can be used to help students organize ideas graphically, and drafts can be typed and edited on the computer.
- Finished products can be published on the class web page for other adolescents to read and critique or respond to, printed in a school publication, and/or sent to an outside firm.
- Adolescents need also to reflect on their own (possibly changed) beliefs about poetry and their ability to make meaning.

*Your
Ideas*

Learning Is Interactive

Current theorists acknowledge that learning is a social process supported through meaningful interaction with resources in the learning environment (Perkins 1992; Resnick 1989). Resnick observed that in real life, mental activity is rarely done without some kind of external assistance, and that classroom environments should facilitate similar interaction. She noted that "human cognition is so varied and sensitive to cultural context" that ways must be found for people to "actively shape each other's knowledge and reasoning processes" (1987, 2). When thinking is socially shared, adolescents' internal mental conversations are made visible and the knowledge they bring to the learning experience can be examined, built upon, strengthened and, if necessary, reshaped. Resnick has referred to this intellectual interaction as shared cognition.

Shared Cognition

The external resources that support adolescent learning may be human, such as the teacher, other students, and other adults, or they may be symbolic tools that enable students to retrieve, manipulate, and organize information. These symbolic supports can include various technologies, such as computers or graphing calculators, or graphic organizers, such as K/NK charts, diagrams, observation reports, sequence chains, decision-making structures, dialectic journals, concept webs, story maps, ranking ladders, flow charts, and analogy links (Daniels and Bizar 1998; Fogarty and Bellanca 1995b). Perkins used the term "person-plus" to explain this purposeful interaction of the learner's inner resources with the range of supports in the learning surroundings (1992, 134). The following examples illustrate.

Visual Organizers

- A teacher can help students compare and contrast the cultures of two Native American groups with a large Venn diagram drawn on the board. This graphic design enables adolescents to view information and organize the knowledge so that differences and similarities are more visually apparent.
- Students can use dialectic journal (divided notebook page) to show problem figuring and mathematical reasoning in trigonometry. This graphic format helps to make their mental processes visible so that they can be examined, expanded, and improved.

Technology

- For the task of evaluating the visual impact of cultural portraiture, students in an art class might visit the Web sites of the Louvre, Tate Gallery, the National Portrait Gallery, and the Metropolitan Museum of Art. In this way, technology gives adolescents an interactive learning experience more authentic and effective than looking in the pages of an art book.
- Students in a health class could use computerized exercise machines to gather data on the impact of aerobic conditioning on heart rate. Technology generates pertinent information easily, thus enabling adolescents to move more quickly to the analysis stage of the research process.

Newspapers

- Students in an economics class can analyze the causes of the stock market crash of 1929 by reading newspaper archive articles and talking with business students at an area college. These print and human resources provide rich historical information and current expertise that contribute to the adolescents' understanding of a complex economic phenomenon.

Non-educators

- An interview with a local author can help adolescents understand the literary elements of setting, characterization, and style. This real-world figure provides a credible and authentic resource as they learn first-hand through the words of a literary expert.

Peers

- A teacher could arrange a tutoring partnership between students in two levels of math classes.
- Other students might share perspectives with teens in Japan on world trade negotiations. When adolescents can share or exchange ideas with peers who share new knowledge or alternative ideas, their thinking is challenged and their learning expands.

Your Ideas

especially when students teach each other.

Distributed Intelligence

A phenomenon closely linked with the concept of shared cognition is distributed intelligence (Pea 1993). Gardner theorized that knowledge is distributed. Instead of residing "exclusively within the head of an individual . . . it emerges jointly from one's own perspective, the perspectives of others, and the information that is derived from available

Your Ideas

human and technical resources" (1999, 98). When adolescents are permitted to interact cognitively with peers and to capitalize on other available resources in and beyond the classroom, their learning is expanded and enriched.

Zone of Proximal Development

Of renewed interest among educators has been Vygotsky's (1978) concept of zone of proximal development. This idea suggests that when adolescents are guided by teachers or other competent adults, when they collaborate with more capable peers, or when they are assisted by pertinent learning devices, they can achieve a level of competence beyond what they would have reached on their own (Bransford et al. 1999). The intentional sharing of expertise in the learning community provides a form of intellectual scaffolding that both supports and challenges adolescents to move progressively toward deeper understanding and more independent learning.

Learning As Thinking About Knowledge

Central to current theoretical agreement is the importance of knowledge and how it is constructed during the learning process. Learning depends on the way adolescents deal internally and externally with knowledge (Resnick 1999b). The construction of knowledge and the acquisition of cognitive strategies to process information and solve problems is critical in this era of information explosion (Resnick 1999b). Thoughtful learning, however, is more than simply adding, expanding, organizing, and reorganizing cognitive structures, as viewed by the information-processing theorists of past decades (Bransford et al. 1999; Perkins 1992). Memory is important, yet knowledge needs to be related, extended, refined, and applied to new situations (Marzano et al. 1992). The rapid cellular transactions that take place when such connections are made strengthen adolescents' understanding and provide a stronger knowledge base for future learning (Caine and Caine 1997; Jensen 1998).

For adolescents to think about knowledge in a thoughtful way, four conditions should be in place (Bransford et al. 1999; Caine and Caine 1997; Jensen, 1998; Perkins 1992).

1. The knowledge needs to be substantive and considered "worthy" of adolescent thought. Though the attainment of facts or isolated information may be necessary in certain instances, adolescents' minds are more likely to relate to the broader ideas with which they can grapple or the intriguing problems that they can approach.

2. Adolescents should be expected to think critically about the knowledge they are acquiring. While adolescents need a solid foundation of basics—formulas, theorems, steps, principles—they need to interact with the knowledge in a meaningful way. They should question, apply, compare, adapt, speculate, analyze, synthesize, hypothesize, and draw conclusions about information.

3. Adolescents need an opportunity to construct an understanding of the knowledge in collaboration with others, including the teacher. Intentional and sustained interaction with supporting resources in the learning environment strengthens learning. Adolescents' knowledge base broadens as expertise is shared through collaboration.

4. The classroom climate should be conducive to intellectual, social, and emotional growth. In a learning environment where adolescents feel individually valued, accepted, and challenged, they will take a risk with higher-level thinking, rise to a teacher's expectations, and progress toward improved thinking and understanding.

The Social-Emotional Context

Adolescents often give the impression that they are secure, confident, calm, in command, and in need of no one, when in actuality, they may be dealing with a range of emotions: *How do I fit in? How can I fit in? How dumb does that sound? I know I can't do this. I hope no one finds out what I'm really feeling. I wish I could be more . . . I wish I could be more like . . .* Their internal thoughts are preoccupied with questions about personal and social identity, yet they try hard to project an image of self-assuredness. As discussed in chapter 2, the way adolescents feel about themselves and how they are perceived by others affects their learning.

While current theorists propose that learning is an active process enhanced through social interaction, they also agree that classrooms are not emotionally neutral places (Wolfe and Brandt 1998). Adolescents' feelings, emotions, beliefs, and perceptions affect how they interact with each other, the attitude they have in general toward learning, and their motivation to commit to its challenge. "[L]earning is enhanced when the environment provides the opportunity to discuss their thinking out loud, to bounce their ideas off peers, and to produce collaborative work" (Wolfe and Brandt 1998, 11). Adolescents need a learning context where personal competence is nurtured, emotions are positively stimulated, and social interaction is carefully structured.

Your Ideas

Your Ideas

Figure 4.2 synthesizes current ideas for fostering positive social-emotional support as espoused by many scholars including Diamond and Hopson (1998), Jensen (1998), and Goleman (1995). Examples are given in the following section.

Building Social-Emotional Support

1. Personalize Learning Opportunities.

Differentiate curriculum for varying abilities and interests.
Permit choice on topics, projects and resources.
Assess understanding through multiple avenues.
Design authentic and developmentally challenging experiences.
Allow for creativity and originality.
Integrate music, art, and drama to promote individual expression.
Give adolescents opportunities to "shine."

2. Build Relationships.

Provide opportunities for peer interaction.
Structure collaborative tasks and monitor group dynamics.
Teach interpersonal skills (e.g., team and consensus building).
Provide opportunity for community connections and social action.
Involve families.

3. Promote Inner Management.

Build in metacognitive time (e.g., reflection, discussion, response writing, self-evaluation).
Foster empathy (e.g., perspective-taking, debate, role playing).
Encourage moral development (e.g., decision-making, discussion, inquiry projects)
Treat mistakes as learning experiences and emphasize personal progress.
Provide opportunities for learning responsibility and ownership.
Involve classroom management planning and conflict negotiation.
Downplay extrinsic motivation and promote the value of learning.

4. Create Emotional Security.

Promote a climate of caring, respect, inclusiveness, and acceptance.
Create an atmosphere of expectancy, challenge, and limited stress.
Listen to and help them believe in the power of their ideas.
Encourage efforts to understand and to be understood.
Celebrate classroom cultures and discourage prejudice.
Incorporate humor and playfulness.

5. Teach Well.

Capture curiosity through a challenging curriculum (e.g., concepts, issues, problems).
Help adolescents to see the practicality of what they are learning.
Expect adolescents to be active participants, not passive listeners.
Foster thoughtful learning and understanding.
Expand the "walls" of the classroom through technology and external resources.

Figure 4.2

Personalize Learning Opportunities

Your Ideas

Positive social-emotional development is promoted when adolescents are allowed to learn and to show their learning in multiple ways, when they are given choices and opportunity for input, or when they are encouraged to express individual talents, to share original ideas, or to pursue areas of interest. Teachers can plan instruction that differentiates and personalizes for adolescent learners, as the following examples illustrate:

- A teacher might use a character trait strategy based on Steven Covey's book, *The Seven Habits of Highly Effective People* (1989). Students are given a list of traits, including tolerant, trustworthy, problem solving, diligent, kind, courageous, peaceful, and resourceful. Both teacher and students select three they hope others would use to describe them, and discuss, write, role play, and create desk posters. Whenever students engage in inappropriate behavior, they are asked to explain how their actions are consistent (Fleming 1996).

- A middle school teacher can help students balance between "outersense" (the way they interact with others) and "innersense" (their individuality) through journaling, seminars, conferences, and personal style questionnaires. A study of the Ennegram, a 2000-year-old tool used as a rite of passage in tribal cultures can help them understand their identity and role (Shelton 1999).

- Students in a literature class might choose how they do book reports. Selections could include dramatic skits, book talks, poetry, or musical compositions.

Creating Connections and Building Relationships

Adolescent social-emotional development is enhanced when teachers provide opportunities for interpersonal networking and relationship building. Learning experiences that require cooperation, collaboration, and consensus or realistic problems that enable connections and extensions beyond the classroom foster a healthy sense of community. A few examples illustrate.

- Middle school students might decide to get involved in the local humane society's effort to take care of orphaned animals. They could wash the animals, build shelters, and assist in placing the animals in adoptive homes.

*Your
Ideas*

- High school students might be paired with mentors at a local university. They could meet in small advisory groups of ten to twelve to plan exhibitions and projects (Littky and Allen 1999).
- Language arts students can keep portfolios and assume responsibility for leading parent conferences.

Promoting Inner Management

Teachers provide support for social-emotional development when they create opportunities for adolescents to think about and take responsibility for personal viewpoints, decisions, and actions. By grappling with the perspectives of others, talking through conflict, or reflecting on personal learning progress, adolescents can begin to develop a more integrated and intrinsically motivated sense of self. For example

- A math teacher can turn the teaching over to a student. The student might demonstrate a problem on the chalkboard while the teacher sits in a classroom desk, models question posing, and takes notes in a learning log (Schneider 1996).
- A teacher might use the StePs model (Structured Team Problem Solving) during class meetings to negotiate everyday conflicts, such as how to deal with cliques, stealing, or cheating. Led by a classmate, adolescents brainstorm ideas for solutions, cluster and clarify them, and create graphic visuals to show their thoughts (Metivier and Sheive 1990; Schneider 1996).
- Students can discuss the meaning of logical consequences in terms of the four Rs: relate logically to the behavior, be reasonable by focusing on the immediate event, respect the student's dignity, and allow the student to be responsible for personal actions (Evans 1996).
- From time to time, a teacher might audiotape the classroom. Students can listen to the tone of the dialogue and screen for "killer statements" by both teacher and students, such as, "That's a dumb question" (Frieberg 1996).

Creating Emotional Security

A climate of caring, respect, and acceptance is critical to positive adolescent social-emotional development. Stress caused by prejudice or exclusiveness should be eliminated, and challenge promoted by high expectations for all students should be apparent.

- A teacher might periodically ask students to fill out an evaluation form. Questions could include, Do I treat students with respect?

Am I sensitive to students' needs? Do students feel comfortable asking questions? Are students actively interested in class work? Is enough time given for tasks? (Belton 1996).

Your Ideas

- A middle school teacher and students might craft a class constitution. In small groups students can discuss ideas for an ideal society. Suggestions are presented, and the class talks about problems faced by current society. Each student writes five rules that will help prepare for the kind of society they envision. These rules are categorized, a preamble drafted, and non-punitive interventions detailed for those not abiding by the covenant. Rules might include listening to each other's ideas, treating with fairness, speaking and acting in non-embarrassing ways, and maintaining orderly personal habits. Consequences might include verbal and written reminders, a class meeting, and a meeting with parents or the principal (Fleming 1996).

- Before a class debate in social studies a teacher can remind students of several ground rules. These might include the following:
  - listen to others' perspectives;
  - present your views with clarity; and
  - support your ideas with reasoning.

- On a weekly basis a class can engage in a twenty-minute seminar on various topics generated by students. Sessions might include dealing with conflict at home, peer pressure, social relationships, death, and school violence. Teachers can also use bibliotherapy, in which novels are selected for discussion based on problems adolescents face in their personal lives.

Teaching Well

Perhaps most valuable in building positive social-emotional support for adolescents is good instruction. Relevant, meaningful, and broadly interactive learning experiences that stimulate adolescents' curiosity, challenge their thinking, and promote understanding enable them to develop intellectually, personally, and socially. A couple of examples follow:

- Adolescents are fascinated by the mummification process and early views of the afterlife, and they enjoy myths and folklore. In part of an in-depth study of ancient Egyptian culture, students might select and assume the role of an early figure (e.g., political leader, slave, farmer's wife, high priest, young student). They can research through various sources to create a first-person data sheet. Questions could include, What is your level of education

and how is it impacted by your social status? How is what you eat affected by the economics of your family? Students should also be allowed to add personal interest questions (Tomlinson 1999).

- With the continuing debate over the health risk of tobacco, the lure of youth through targeted advertisement, and the discussion at the national level to declare tobacco a drug, a teacher might pose this challenge: You have been asked by the Office of the Surgeon General to design an anti-smoking ad campaign geared to adolescents. Students can collaborate to develop a peer survey to find out reasons for smoking. They can conduct research on the accompanying health hazards and work in teams to design a marketable plan. Each team can evaluates how well they work together and how they might improve collaborative skills.

Theorists agree that learning is an active and interactive process of meaningful knowledge construction affected by many interacting factors internal to the adolescents and external in learning context. Adolescents' brains actively hunger for meaning, yet they relate better when confronted with realistic and challenging experiences that motivate them to use their higher thinking capacities (Tomlinson 1999). Knowledge expands and enriches through a concerted sharing of ideas, and it is corrected and shaped into understanding through guidance, feedback, and reflection. The teacher plays a critical role in facilitating a resourceful, challenging, and responsive environment that enables adolescents to be cognitively active, personally motivated, and interpersonally engaged. In this environment, learning is thoughtful and deep conceptual understanding is possible.

Schooling Minds Not Memories

Knowledge appears to be highly prized in schools, but in many instances it is not the kind that helps adolescents relate to and understand their world, and it is generally not the kind that endures. David Perkins (1991) expressed concern that many teachers use what he called a "chocolate box" model of learning. They keep trying to add pieces of differently flavored chocolates into the "candy box of the mind," but do not teach for deeper understanding. He has whimsically referred to "inert" information that cannot be recalled or used meaningfully, as the "couch potato" equivalent of knowledge: "It's there, but it doesn't move around or do anything" (1991, 22).

In his book, *Knowledge as Design* (1986), Perkins wrote that too much of what is taught in schools is "disconnected knowledge," or information that has no context, critical perspective, or application.

Historical dates and facts are learned, for example, without connection
to the milestone events that shape history. Analogies are not often
drawn to present-day occurrences and varying perspectives are not
examined. Without a link to thinking, facts are like "threads without a
tapestry"; they remain meaningless and abstract, and are not flexible
and functional in adolescents' lives (1986, 22). Focused more on
schooling the memory than schooling the mind, this so-called learning
is frequently antithetical to knowledge retention and understanding.

*Your
Ideas*

Other educators have expressed similar concerns about "naïve"
and "ritualistic" knowledge in students (Brooks, J. G. and Brooks, M. G.
1993; Gardner 1991; Roth 1990). Naive knowledge surfaces, for example, in adolescents' misconceptions about why an object sinks or floats,
or that all good poetry must rhyme, or that intelligence is associated
with a particular race or culture. These theories are formed early in life
as they try to make sense of what they see in their world, and are
brought into classroom as inaccurate beliefs (Gardner 1991, 1999).
"Ritualistic" knowledge amasses with the rote memorization of information without knowing what it means. Students might learn the textbook
definition of photosynthesis, for example, or think that percentage calculation merely means to move a decimal point two places.

Teaching to the memory and not the mind is antithetical to
thoughtful learning (Perkins, 1999). It is an amassing of information
that merely sits in the mind's attic gathering dust. Having memorized
the steps necessary for a bill to become a law, for example, does not
mean that a student will be able to name them a week later or that he
or she understands the political complexity that unfolds during a bill's
debate on the floor of the Senate. Moreover, correctly listing these
steps on a unit test does not guarantee that the adolescent will see a
relationship to the ongoing legislative debate over immigration quotas
or the connection between the legislative process. Teaching to the
memory and not the mind also affects the possibility for knowledge to
be transferred to other situations or used later in life.

Knowledge Under Construction

How can teachers facilitate and guide productive knowledge construction? How can the "couch potato" syndrome be shaken, inaccurate
assumptions be corrected, or complex principles, definitions, and procedures be better understood? The ACT Model, "Seeing is Believing,"
provides an example. The instructional intent is to help students understand the interrelationship of gravity, velocity, acceleration, and distance on falling objects. Adolescents tend to hold fast to the misconcep-

*Your
Ideas*

tion that heavier objects fall faster than lighter ones, and even when told differently, many fail to understand the complex relationship among density, velocity, acceleration, and gravity. The learning goals are to (1) dispel any "naïve" assumptions; (2) help students construct a conceptual understanding of the law of falling bodies; and (3) help them recognize these principles in their own lives.

Knowledge Under Construction: Seeing is Believing

Many adolescents have naïve or incorrect beliefs about natural phenomena related to certain principles of physics, including the concepts of motion, gravity, density, velocity, and mass as they relate to falling objects. Teachers can challenge these assumptions through inquiry, experimentation, and reflective discussion. This instructional approach helps adolescents to construct a more accurate knowledge base that can enable genuine understanding.

Content Understanding

To help adolescents understand the principles of motion and the nature of scientific inquiry.

Strategies for Inquiry

An Inquiry Statement: If you drop two objects of different weights from the same height, they will hit the ground simultaneously.

- ■ The teacher can ask students to respond on a note card in one of three ways (True, False, It All Depends) to the above question. On the back of the card, students should provide an explanation.

- ■ Students can then compare responses with a partner and share with the class while the teacher records speculations on a board chart. A sample follows.

True	False	It All Depends
Gravity pulls both equally.	The heavier would hit first.	If the weights are really close.
They must weigh the same.	The heavier would gain speed.	If the distance is not very high.

- ■ The teacher can use guided questioning to discuss students' perceptions. Strategic questions might include
    - – Would it matter if the same objects were dropped inside or outside?
    - – How might the wind make a difference?
    - – What if there was absolutely no resistance, for example, in a vacuum?
    - – How can we test the validity of your ideas?

Guided Interaction

■ The teacher can guide as small groups of students determine and conduct a series of experiments in which differently weighted objects (feathers, golf balls, tennis balls, and basketballs) are dropped from various heights (the stadium seats, gym balcony, an outside ramp). Team members should discuss and record observations about size, weight and height.

■ When the class is reconvened, students can be asked to interpret findings, observations, and reasoning about gravity and air resistance.

■ The teacher should introduce the terms velocity (the speed an object falls through the air) and density (its weight).

Cross-Disciplinary Applications

■ Students could open a small traveler's bag that contains such items as a newspaper announcing the end of World War II, a Chicago map, a tube of red lipstick, two chocolate bars, a hair net, a small diary, and a Hemingway novel. They could be asked to construct an understanding of the culture (values, interests, life style) and times of the person through the clues and ensuing investigation.

■ Following a nature walk in the fall during which seeds are collected, students can be asked to consider why the seeds "wait" until spring to germinate. They could speculate what happens to seeds during the course of winter and hypothesize the most favorable conditions for germination. These can then be tested through classroom simulations, including variation of temperature, fire, water, acid, (as in animals' stomachs,) or "crunching" (as under human feet).

■ Students could design hot air balloons from panels of glued tissue paper, speculate about height and conditions for flight, and test assumptions by launching the creations using a stovepipe fashioned heater fueled by pine cones.

Metacognitive Development and Assessment

For extended inquiry, the teacher can pose other hypothetical questions, such as

> If you reason that force of gravity is so strong, even on objects of a different density, what would you say about two objects of the same density but of different shapes?

■ Students can apply the scientific process by generating hypotheses and designing additional experiments to test ideas. These experiments might include dropping flat and crumpled pieces of paper from the same height. Others might be designed to determine if falling bodies are affected by horizontal motion during descent or if distance has an impact on speed of the fall. Observations should be recorded, data analyzed, and conclusions drawn and shared with other teams. The teacher should ask for "constructed" definitions of other terms, such as acceleration.

■ The teacher can promote transfer by asking students to think of examples in real life where these forces of physics are evident. Questions can be raised about flight, for example, and speculations ventured as to whether a glider and a jet, in the absence of air, will fall to the ground at the same speed from the same height. Questions can be posed about weightlessness, space travel, and the gravitational relationship of the moon to the earth.

■ As a performance assessment, students can design word problems using the concepts of acceleration, velocity, and density, which can be tested with computer simulations.

Constructivism

In a recent journal article, Perkins (1999) recognized constructivism as a philosophy that promotes thoughtful learning in the classroom. He noted three basic learning premises that undergird the constructivist instructional approach. These are

1. Knowledge and understanding are actively acquired. Depending on the situation, students might experiment, discuss, assume a role, debate, or investigate.

- In history class, students could describe an event during the French Revolution by writing a letter from the viewpoint of a French aristocrat to someone in another country.
- In language arts class, students might relate a poem to an event in their lives.
- In science, students could gather samples from an estuary to test salinity composition and speculate about sea life and habitation.
- In math, students might learn statistics by analyzing beverage consumption data to determine the best market location for a new soft drink industry.

2. Knowledge and understanding are socially constructed in dialogue with others. The role of questioning and making thinking "visible" through response helps teachers determine adolescents' prior knowledge and ongoing understanding.

- In the ACT, "Knowledge Under Construction," students are helped to "construct" a better understanding of the scientific principles related to falling objects. They speculate, test hypotheses, discuss findings, and are challenged by questions for extended inquiry.

3. Knowledge and understanding are created and recreated. Adolescents are unlikely to develop understanding with one example or one experiment. Learning needs to be reinforced and applied in a variety of ways.

- The teacher's questions in the "Knowledge Under Construction" ACT model do not allow students to stop with an incomplete understanding of gravitational pull. They interject horizontal motion and density, and help students make connections with flight. Students should better retain what they learn and more readily recognize other examples in their own lives.

In the future, adolescents will need to examine large bodies of information and, according to Gardner, "determine what is worth knowing" (1999, 53). They should know how to think critically. They will not develop this intellectual capacity, however, by memorizing disconnected information or by parroting definitions meaninglessly. Adolescents learn through thinking, but they need to be taught to think for understanding.

Your
Ideas

Promoting Thinking Development

For adolescents to become better thinkers, they must be immersed in settings where thinking drives the understanding of knowledge. In their book, *The Thinking Classroom*, Shari Tishman, David Perkins, and Eileen Jay described a thinking culture as one where the language, values, expectations, and habits support an "enterprise of good thinking" (1995, 22). They identified several dimensions of classroom life conducive to thinking development. They emphasized initially that teachers and students should be familiar with and use vocabulary and terms that convey the thinking process or goal. The following examples illustrate.

- A teacher might use the terms hypothesize, test assumptions, experiment, analyze findings, and draw conclusions.
- A social studies teacher might ask a student to think from an alternate perspective.
- A language arts teacher could use such words as characterize, infer, interpret, justify, and explain during a drama and poetry discussion.
- An art teacher might use the terms observe, critique, appraise, investigate, and compare.

Teachers need to speak the language of thinking, write the terms on charts in the room, demonstrate what they mean, and help adolescents recognize when they are using the skill appropriately and well. Students need to develop mental models of what higher-level thinking is and sounds like for the skills to be internalized. They need to hear and use thinking language within the context of ongoing learning experiences. Figure 4.3 suggests some of the thinking terminology that can be used within and across disciplines as first enunciated by Bloom (1956) and later refined by Tishman, Perkins, and Jay (1995) along with others.

Thinking classrooms are also places where adolescents and teachers place high value on thinking well (Tishman et al. 1995). Students learn to discern between good and shallow reasoning, for example, or they recognize that open-mindedness can minimize premature judgment. The dispositions for and habits of intelligent thinking, however, often have to be taught. Figure 4.4 follows a discussion of the short story, "The Lottery" (Jackson 1966), in a language arts class. The teacher's questioning is designed to help students recognize the nature

The Language of Thinking

Literary Meaning	Mathematical Reasoning	Scientific Inquiry	Historical Analysis	Artistic Expression
Infer	Subdivide	Speculate/Research	Investigate	Review/Scrutinize
Discern	Solve	Suggest/Suppose	Corroborate	Select
Hypothesize	Prove	Surmise/Theorize	Reflect/Establish	Recreate
Interpret/Contend	Detect/Scrutinize	Reason	Convince/Dissent	Understand
Dissent/Consider	Weigh/Conjecture	Prove	Attest	Recognize/Perceive
Conclude/Question	Dissect	Probe	Affirm	Realize/Appreciate
Ponder	Derive/Ascertain	Propose/Postulate	Explore	Muse
Predict	Calculate/Assess	Analyze/Dispute	Inquire/Suppose	Observe/Evaluate
Opine/Summarize	Comprehend	Examine/Construe	Remember/Rebut	Relate
Perceive	Deduce	Assess	Maintain/Submit	Discriminate
Critique	Demonstrate	Claim	Resolve/Recollect	Differentiate
Relate	Estimate	Confirm/Establish	Study/Restructure	Recommend
Restate	Determine	Justify	Interpret	Describe
Review	State			
Imply	Categorize			
Contrast	Rate			

Figure 4.3

and quality of their thinking expression. A classroom environment that reflects a thoughtfulness of both spirit and mind fosters positive thinking dispositions and habit, builds interpersonal relationships, and promotes adolescent cognitive development (Beamon 1997).

Another element important to adolescent thinking development is the use of their metacognitive skills (Barell 1995; Perkins 1992; Tishman, Perkins, and Jay 1995). Adolescents need multiple opportunities to make their thinking visible. Fogarty and Bellanca have distinguished three phases of metacognitive practice: planning, monitoring, and evaluating (1995b, 84-85). At the onset of an activity, adolescents should articulate what they are trying or need to do; during a task, they should stop periodically to check their progress; and at the completion, they should look back and assess how well they did. Ultimately, adolescents need to learn to organize their thinking by conscious strategy and to get in the habit of pondering how it can be improved. A few examples of instructional strategies that promote metacognitive thinking follow.

Think Aloud A teacher can pair students for a "think aloud" technique for mathematical problem solving. One student assumes the role of problem solver by thinking aloud as he or she works through the problem. The second student acts as monitor who asks questions to prompt thinking (Fogarty and Bellanca 1995; Whimbey 1975).

*Your
Ideas*

Self-Evaluation

Following inquiry projects, a teacher might give each group of students an evaluation form with these questions:

- What strategies did you use to organize the investigation?
- What resources were most useful?
- What were any problems that arose?
- What factored into your decision for presentation format?
- How well did your group cooperate?
- What different strategies might you have used?

Individual Reflections Chemistry students might be required to write individual reflections after each lab experiment that critique the procedures used.

Stop-n-Write Periodically during a discussion of a controversial issue in social studies, a teacher might pause for students to "stop-n-write" their ongoing reactions on paper (Daniels and Bizar 1998).

Three Questions In preparation for seminars, a teacher might have students write down three questions they have about the reading.

Learning Logs Students might be asked to keep learning logs to reflect on their daily progress in understanding concepts in science (Daniels and Bizar 1998).

Adolescent thinking is also promoted in a classroom where the focus is on higher-level knowledge development, problem solving, and inquiry (Tishman et al. 1995). Resnick (1999b) has emphasized that learning is knowledge-dependent, while others, including Gardner (1999), Paul (1998), Perkins (1992), and Wiggins and McTigue (1998), have stressed that conceptual understanding comes when students think critically and collaboratively about higher-order knowledge. Each content area has certain foundational principles and skills that should be learned, such as mathematical formulas and basic operations, scientific principles and methods of inquiry, or historical timelines, and literary language. Each area also has enduring questions that inspire inquiry, strategies that direct problem solving, and a specific way of thinking about knowledge. Learning experiences that help adolescents think more as disciplinary experts can help them understand the higher-order knowledge at the core of a discipline (Bransford et al. 1999).

Your Ideas

Figure 4.4 gives examples of specific disciplinary thinking and offers a few instructional suggestions that promote inquiry and problem solving. These are more fully developed in chapter 5. The following tips for promoting adolescents thinking and higher-order knowledge development are useful for teachers in any content area (Gardner 1991, 1999; Perkins 1992; Tishman et al. 1995).

1. Give adolescents enough time to shape questions, conduct investigations or solve problems.
2. Explain and discuss problem-solving, inquiry, and other thinking strategies.
3. Provide continual feedback, both corrective and supportive, so adolescents can recognize a standard for thinking appropriately within a discipline.
4. Draw from adolescents their own conceptions about conducting inquiry or approaching problems.
5. Promote frequent interaction so adolescents can share ideas, articulate thinking, and reflect on what they are doing and why.
6. Use authentic examples, such as real historical research, scientific discoveries, mathematical problems, and significant literary and artistic works.
7. Enable adolescents to build understanding collaboratively with disciplinary "experts" who have a workable understanding of the skills and content.

A Change in the Teacher-Student Relationship

Teaching for adolescent learning requires a changed relationship among teachers and students. The traditional image of the teacher as disseminator of knowledge and the student as passive recipient does little to promote thoughtful learning and independent thinking (Brown and Campione 1996). How can adolescents learn to reason independently if they are always told what to believe and how to think? How can they learn to deal with the ambiguity of life if the content they face lacks complexity? How can they learn strategies if they do not practice problem solving? How can adolescents learn to formulate pertinent questions, reason logically, make thoughtful decisions, or evaluate personal thinking and its progress without guidance, assistance, and feedback?

Developing Higher-Order Thinking	Instructional Strategies
Historical thinking involves learning to: • identify various historical perspectives • recognize that context and vantage shape interpretation • understand the relationship of past events to current events	**History** • role playing • problem-based learning • simulation • discussion • research projects
Scientific inquiry is shaped through: • testing assumptions based on observations • gathering data • seeking justification • deriving conclusions	**Science** • research projects • experimentation • problem solving • web-based inquiry • scientific method • problem-based learning
Mathematical thinking involves: • problem solving • deductive reasoning • systematic logic	**Mathematics** • word problems • learning journals • dialectic journals • problem posing • authentic data analysis
Literary thinking involves: • making inferences about meaning and interpretation • checking for textual evidence • substantiating ideas • organizing for expression or argument	**Language Arts** • seminar • questioning • persuasive writing • debate • synthesis papers • presentation • perspective writing
Thinking in the fine arts involves: • sensory observation • critical listening • comparative analysis • inquiry	**Fine Arts** • dramatic performance • musical composition • creative design • visual analysis • presentation • research

Figure 4.4

One metaphor used to describe teachers' new role is cognitive or metacognitive coach (Center for Problem-Based Learning 1996; Gallagher 1997; Perkins 1991, 1992). Gavriel Saloman has referred to this relationship between classroom "coach" and students as "partners in cognition" (Saloman, Perkins, and Globerson 1991). The suggested interaction between teacher and students is illustrated in the ACT

Model, "A Cognitive/Metacognitive Coaching Model." The teacher guides adolescents' thinking about the task through purposeful questioning, helps them to generate a K/NK board to organize their ideas, and assists as they determine strategy and course of action. The teacher also helps students prioritize findings, make decisions for the proposal, draw closure, and think about their learning. Later in the application, the teacher assists in preparation for the proposal and allows time for reflection and evaluation on the process. Figures 4.5 and 4.6 detail possible student ideas for a K/KN board and show a task structure analysis respectively.

The teacher's role in the learning environment is strategically important. As facilitators, teachers plan and manage opportunities for adolescents to interact, make decisions, ask questions, and problem-solve. They model and coach, probe and challenge, guide and monitor, motivate and encourage, expect and hold accountable, and assess and prompt. They carefully orchestrate the opportunity for adolescents to grow intellectually, socially, and personally.

A Cognitive/Metacognitive Coaching Model: A Question of Priority

Adolescents are often concerned when natural disasters affect the lives of human and animals and the quality of their environment. Authentic problems based on real disasters, such as determining relief funding for the victims of hurricane-induced flooding, can be designed. These learning experiences promote and extend inquiry into real-world events and help adolescents broaden personal perspectives.

Content Understanding

To promote an awareness of civic responsibility and help students develop inquiry skills for real-world problem solving.

Strategies for Inquiry

An Inquiry Challenge: The devastation from the hurricane flooding in a southeastern state has drawn national attention. The president of the United States has asked the governor to submit a proposal to the Federal Disaster Relief Agency to quality for funding up to $10 million. This plan must specify how the relief money would be used for area reconstruction and to safeguard the eastern region against future flooding disasters. You have been asked by the Governor to serve on a team of investigators to develop this proposal. The plan should address the most pressing human and environmental needs in the flood-stricken area and be written in priority order.

■ The teacher should guide students in the development of a "Know/Need to Know" board (see Figure 4.5). This graphic organizer will help students to (1) define the problem or task situation; (2) formulate inquiry questions; (3) identify needed information and resources; and (4) determine a course of investigative action.

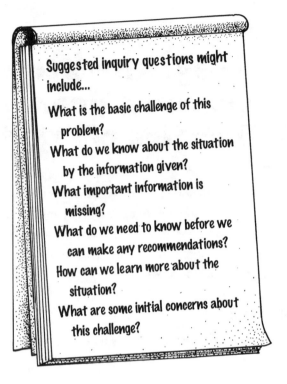

Suggested inquiry questions might include...

What is the basic challenge of this problem?

What do we know about the situation by the information given?

What important information is missing?

What do we need to know before we can make any recommendations?

How can we learn more about the situation?

What are some initial concerns about this challenge?

Guided Interaction

- The teacher will guide as students determine a course of action to address the problem. Inquiry teams with designated tasks can be formed. Reference to the K/KN board can help students in the choice of areas for investigative focus

- The teacher should also facilitate as students identify resources, determine strategy, generate research questions, and develop a reasonable time line for the inquiry. A task structure analysis chart will be useful to organize strategy.

- The teacher will also need to assist as teams reconvene and collaborate to prioritize findings to make the funding recommendation.

Metacognitive Development and Assessment

- The teacher should monitor as investigative teams implement strategies and tap resources. Progress should be checked systematically through written status reports and questioning. At times, adolescents may have to rethink and change strategy.

- Students should be included in the discussion of criteria for and format of the final product.

These criteria might include

- accuracy of information
- prioritization based on supporting rationale
- professional format of report.
- group collaboration and individual contribution should also be evaluated.

To promote further authenticity, local or state officials or selected public figures can assume a role in the evaluation process. A review panel might be assembled, a teleconference arranged, or the report mailed to an external source for feedback.

Time should be provided for reflection at the close of the simulation. The problem-solving strategies and their implication for other real-world situations can be discussed.

Cross Disciplinary Applications

- A newspaper is an excellent source for current events that can be shaped into ill-structured problems. The ongoing debate over money for space travel; the use of DNA for prosecution of alleged criminals; human cloning; nuclear disarmament; animal rights concerns; and environmental protection issues are a few ideas that might appeal to the adolescent audience.

- Literature also provides a rich source material for inquiry. As a prelude to reading Arthur Miller's *The Crucible*, for example, a teacher might pose this problem:

It is the year 1692 in Salem, Massachusetts. The news has spread among the townspeople that a young slave girl named Tituba has confessed to witchcraft and is to be hanged at Gallow Hill. Rumors are also circulating that the girl is innocent . . .

A Know/Need to Know (K/KN) Board for Inquiry-Based Learning

What is the challenge?

The Govenor has commissioned a proposal for federal relief.
The plan must indicate proposed use for $10 million funding.
The proposal must prioritize the areas' greatest needs.
The plan must be future-oriented.

What Do We Know?	What Do We Need to Know?	How Will We Find Out?
Eastern NC needs funding.	What are the greatest needs?	Find out details about damage.
Hurricanes have caused massive flooding.	What relief efforts have begun?	Learn about flood control.
The proposal must indicate need.	Has any money been given by other agencies?	Find out what efforts have begun.
The proposal must have a plan for use of funding.	What is the extent of the damage for area people?	Learn the extent of crop damage. Learn about the chemicals in flood run-off.
The plan is for a limited amount.	How much has insurance helped?	Learn about disaster insurance.
The plan must prioritize needs.	Are people still displaced?	Find out about interest groups.
Decisions must be made about where money is most needed.	What is the damage to area crops?	Learn about life in estuaries.
There will not be enough for all people wanting money.	How have farmers suffered?	Learn about federal funding in related disasters.
Everyone's needs can't be met.	What about pollution in streams?	Learn about long-term effects of corrosion on farm land.
Consideration must be given to people, plant/animal life and the natural environment.	Has pollution reached the ocean? What will be the long-term impact on plant and animal life in estuaries?	Find out about efforts to combat pollution in streams.
The Govenor and state are depending on us.	What is the impact on environment?	Find out about COSTS!
This problem is HARD!	What interest groups are competing for funding?	Find out about other sources for federal funding.

Figure 4.5

Cognitive Apprenticeship and Adolescent Learning

This new relationship among teachers and adolescent learners has also been referred to as cognitive apprenticeship (Collins, Beranek, and Newman 1991; Collins, Brown, and Newman 1989). In his book, *The Unschooled Mind: How Children Think and How Schools Should*

A Task Structure Analysis for Team Investigation

	Team 1	Team 2	Team3	Team 4	Team 5
Inquiry Task	Status of environmental damage from run-off pollution; Costs for reconstruction.	Extent of damage to area farm industry (e.g., crops, livestock); Costs for reconstruction.	Impact on people (homes, property, insurance); Current status: displacement and assistance.	Techniques and costs of flood control efforts; Other possible money sources.	Other federally funded initiatives, esp. for flooding and hurricane disasters.
Resources	Newspaper Archives, Environmental Agency, Internet Sites (e.g., chemical pollution, estuary life)	Local farmers, Chamber of Commerce, Agricultural Agency, Newspapers	Local Citizens and Officials, Insurance Agencies	Internet (e.g., flood, conservation experts)	
Strategies	Interviews, videotaping, field notes	Phone calls, site visits, taped testimonials	Visits to relief shelters		

Figure 4.6

Teach, Gardner (1991) described the historical significance of an apprenticeship model. It enables young people to work closely with more advanced "experts" in the field. It helps young "novices" to continually improve their skills. This interaction further leads to a product or performance important within a society (1991, 124). In the school setting, an apprenticeship relationship among teachers, students, and others has the advantage of helping adolescents think strategically about knowledge while they progressively strengthen cognitive skills.

Cognitive apprenticeship typically includes the following features (Collins, Brown, and Newman 1989; Ormond 1999):

- Modeling—sudents observe/listen while the teacher demonstrates/explains a task.
- Coaching—students perform the task while the teacher supports with hints/suggestions.
- Sequencing—more challenging/diverse tasks are given as proficiency is gained.

- Externalizing—students explain aloud their knowledge, thinking, and reasoning.
- Reflecting—students compare their thinking and performance with that of "experts."
- Exploring—students are helped to apply/expand/refine the skills independently.

In cognitive apprenticeship, adolescents learn skills and acquire knowledge as they observe and practice under the guidance of a teacher, and they become successively more accomplished (Collins, Brown, and Newman 1989). The focus is on the mental processes used by experts in the discipline to solve complex problems or work through difficult tasks. The expert thinking thus becomes the standard that students strive to approximate. Both teachers and adolescents articulate their thinking processes, and students receive continual feedback and support (scaffolding) from the teacher. Students monitor and evaluate their own progress, make adjustments when improvement is needed, and incrementally develop competence. In the final stages, the teacher gives less assistance, referred to as fading, and students assume more responsibility.

These examples illustrate:

- A mathematics teacher might guide students through the steps of a complex mathematical equation, verbalizing aloud his or her own reasoning. Students can divide their papers into columns. In the left hand columns they work additional problems, and in the right, they record their reasoning processes. They can later explain and compare their strategies with those of other students.
- A language arts teacher might help adolescents develop more sophisticated writing skills with prompt questions used by expert writers. Do I need a stronger transition between these two paragraphs? Would a different word choice communicate better what I want? Do I need to add more reasons to justify my view on the issue?

The goals of metacognitive coaching and cognitive apprenticeship are to help adolescents acquire the knowledge and skills needed for independent thinking and learning. Instructional strategies might include reciprocal teaching, procedural writing, mathematical problem-solving, project-based learning, and problem-based learning (Cognition and Technology Group 1990; Gallagher, et al., 1995; Palincsar and Brown 1984; Schoenfeld 1985). Within this relationship teachers foster metacognitive development by guiding and helping adolescents to think reflectively about personal learning, to monitor and improve skills, and increasingly to assume more control. The graphic in Figure 4.7 depicts

Guiding Toward Metacognitive Management

Your Ideas

The Teacher's Role

verbalizes thinking	guides, questions	becomes less directive (fades)
asks questions	helps with resources	connects to other situations
helps define task	monitors progress	facilitates reflection
structures groups	assists as resource	evaluates learning
helps shape strategy		

METACOGNITIVE GROWTH →

The Adolescent's Role

watches, listens	designs inquiry	evaluates learning
verbalizes conceptions	implements strategy	reflects on process
poses questions	checks personal progress	makes learning connections
suggests strategy	reconsiders strategy	assumes future responsibility

Figure 4.7

this progression from dependence on the teacher's structured guidance to a more independent relationship in which adolescents rely more confidently and competently on their own power for self-regulation.

Social and Emotional Learning

A recent lead article in *Educational Leadership* (Tell 1999-2000) addressed the challenge of connecting with today's youth. Raising the question Generation what?, the author wrote of the conflicting public perceptions of the twelve- to eighteen-year-old population. Comprised of more than 30 million persons, the first generation of the Internet feels disassociated from the adult world and disconnected from school (Public Agenda 1999). What they say they want most is to be taken seriously and to feel connected with teachers and the larger community (Epstein 1998; Hine 1999; Tell 1999–2000).

Increasingly, teachers of adolescents have assumed the role of social and emotional mentor. Their challenge is to connect with students on a more individualized level, to build interpersonal relationships within the classroom, and to promote a sense of emotional well being in the classroom. Adolescents are a diverse group with differing talents, abilities, and experiences that must be acknowledged for them to learn effectively. While socially-oriented, they frequently lack the interpersonal skills to sustain relationship or to interact purposefully with each other and with adults. Their outward appearances may indicate confidence and control, yet, inwardly they are dealing with a range of egocentric feelings and emotions. They need a teacher's assistance to feel emotionally, intellectually, and socially competent, and they need guidance in developing the skills for self-management.

Sagor wrote that "[i]nstilling positive feelings in students will not result from pep talks or positive self-image assemblies but, rather, from planned educational experiences" (1996, 39). He differentiated between students with resilience and those likely to fail by their feelings of competence, belonging, usefulness, potency, and optimism. These can be engendered in the classroom through experiences that

- provide students with genuine evidence of personal academic success (competence);
- show them that they are members of a community (belonging);
- reinforce feelings that they have made a significant contribution (usefulness); and
- help students feel empowered (potency).

Research-based learning experiences that promote adolescent competence, belonging, usefulness, and empowerment include service learning, authentic assessment, portfolios, student-led conferences, goal setting, cooperative learning, teacher advisory groups, and teaching with various learning styles and strengths in mind (Sagor 1999). Experiences that help teach tolerance, empathy, civility, and moral development include perspective-taking, debate, role playing, decision making, discussion, and civic action projects. Personal reflection can be encouraged through journal writing. A sense of community can be built through collaborative inquiry and technology-enhanced projects.

Social and emotional learning is as important for adolescents as academic learning. In an earlier decade Lightfoot observed, "The feelings of anonymity seem diminished by the personal encounters in classrooms" (1983, 347). At the beginning of a new century, the sentiment remains: "Belonging is something that every adolescent should expect at a school. Belonging, or the right to belong, is a moral right of adolescence" (Sizer, T. and Sizer, N. 1999, 98). Adolescents need and seek support, connection, acceptance, feedback, and guidance from teachers and other adults who can influence the direction of their lives. According to one young person, "'Our generation is hopeful . . . . We have lots of ideas about how to improve our world'" (Tell 1999–2000, 13). Making a connection is critical. Teachers hold the key to adolescent social, emotional, and intellectual learning, and to the quality of their future.

Your
Ideas

A New Pedagogy

Linda Darling-Hammond, noted leader in educational reform, proposed a new paradigm for powerful teaching and thoughtful learning. In her address to an audience of educators at the Fourth Annual Teaching for Intelligence Conference (1999, San Francisco), Darling-Hammond called for an instructional approach that would better meet the learning needs of today's students. She described the traditional approach as outmoded and suggested by contrast a "two-way" pedagogy in which students and teachers work supportively and collaboratively to build knowledge and construct understanding.

Darling-Hammond is joined by other educators, including Gardner (1999), Perkins (1992), and Resnick (1999b), who have called for a new way of teaching that is more responsive to adolescents and better prepares them socially, intellectually, and personally for a challenging future. These writers have urged teachers to be more strategic in their instructional efforts to promote thinking and understanding in classrooms. Much attention has also focused on the traits of successful learners (McCombs and Whisler 1997). Successful learners, for example, take an active role constructing new meaning and understanding. They are strategic thinkers who are familiar with and use a range of thinking and reasoning strategies. They also reflect on how they think and learn, set personal and reasonable goals, determine appropriate strategies, and monitor their own progress as they work toward their learning goals.

The questions in Figure 4.8 synthesize many ideas presented in this chapter and should be useful in teaching adolescents to be more thoughtful learners.

The Purpose and Power of Knowledge

Almost twenty years ago, Gene I. Maeroff, an education writer for the *New York Times*, wrote a book entitled, *Don't Blame the Kids: The Trouble with America's Public Schools*. Concerned with the lack of motivation, declining achievement, and increasing violence in schools across the country, he expressed dismay for the lack of rigor and intellectual challenge. His haunting statement holds true today: "Children who do not learn become adults who do not know" (1982, 71). In this

A New Pedagogy

- Do I build on the relevant knowledge and experiences students bring to class?

- Do I take time to find out if they have accurate and sufficient background knowledge to do an academic task?

- Do I require students to consider information from a variety of sources and disciplines?

- Is the task one that is complex enough or is the problem interesting to my students?

- Is there an opportunity for students to use their strengths to create something that would benefit others?

- Does the experience challenge my students to use higher-level thinking operations, such as hypothesis testing, inquiry, reasoning, interpretation, and synthesis?

- Do I give frequent and informative feedback to guide students as they plan and work through tasks?

- Do I allow students to share ideas with and get feedback from others, including peers and knowledgeable "experts"?

- Do my students feel "safe" to take risks or experiment with varying strategies?

- Do I provide time for students to think back over and evaluate how, what and why they learned?

- Do I help students recognize that other learning strategies might be used in the current context or that a specific strategy might be adapted for a different context?

- Do I give students opportunities to practice and develop new levels of skill and competence?

- Am I an enthusiastic expert in my content area and do I share this with students?

Figure 4.8

new age of unfathomable advancements in the purpose and powerfulness of knowledge, the consequences of "not knowing" or "not knowing how" for adolescents are unimaginable.

Adolescence is a time when hormone-induced unpredictability characterizes a pubescent shift from the security of childhood to the expectancy of an adult world. Adolescents must contend with rapid physical, intellectual, and emotional change as they seek to know who they are to be. They should be "immersed" in meaningful, relevant, and intriguing experiences that challenge their thinking, engage their emotions, and charge them with accountability. They need to believe they are capable and intellectually, socially, and emotionally competent, and they need to be primed for real-life responsibility. Teachers have the power to create an instructional environment where adolescents can grow in both mind and personal spirit.

ACTing
on the Adolescent-Centered Learning Principles Discussed in Chapter 4

Principle	*How I can put it into practice*
❏ Shape a classroom culture of thoughtfulness and learning.	
❏ Use instructional practices that emphasize meaningful knowledge construction, mastery of content, thinking development, and social interactions that promote intelligent behaviors in adolescents.	
❏ Help create connections.	
❏ Foster metacognitive development by guiding and helping students to think reflectively about personal learning, to monitor and improve skills, and to increasingly assume more control.	
❏ Immerse students in meaningful, relevant, and intriguing experiences that challenge their thinking, engage their emotions, and charge them with accountability.	
❏ Help students to believe in their personal, intellectual, and social capacities for learning.	

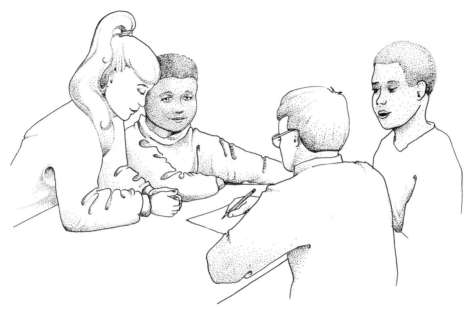

Teaching for Understanding

Seeing Beyond

In Lois Lowry's (1993) Newbery Medal book, *The Giver*, all knowledge of the past is housed in the memory of one person designated as the Receiver. In solitude each day he thinks about this knowledge and ponders its meaning. "It is how wisdom comes," this elder tells young Jonas, who has been selected as the new Receiver. "And how we shape our future" (p. 78). When the memories are shared with Jonas, the lad's world is opened to color and pleasure, and to pain and choice. He acquires self-determination and the personal capacity to see beyond, and his life is never the same.

Teaching for understanding is much like the elder Receiver's gift to Jonas. It enables adolescents to encounter the important ideas that define and shape human existence, and to realize the connecting themes and timeless patterns of the disciplines. It creates a sense of meaning and purpose in a complex data-oriented world. To attain understanding, however, adolescents must confront paradox and ambiguity, and they must deal with imbalance, mystery, and dissonance. In

*Your
Ideas*

this process, their cognitive experiences will be enriched, and they will view themselves, knowledge, and the world differently. Teaching for understanding has the potential to transform. To promote understanding, adolescents should be actively, collaboratively, and intellectually engaged with substantive and enduring content.

Trusting That Less is More

James J. Gallagher, Kenan Professor of Education at the University of North Carolina at Chapel Hill, wrote that the knowledge explosion makes total coverage "an illusion." He urged teachers to consider new instructional approaches that stress "how to access information when it is needed to solve significant problems" (1997, 41). Other educators such as Gardner (1991, 1999), Perkins (1992), and Wiggins and McTigue (1998) have similarly cautioned against the fruitless attempt to try to teach everything in a discipline in the traditional didactic fashion. The body of knowledge in any content area is growing exponentially. It is also difficult to know what information is meaningful for adolescents to know. The following profile gives a snapshot of the current generation of adolescent learners:

- They have known only one Germany.
- The Vietnam War is almost as abstract to them as World War II.
- Many were infants when the Soviet Union dissolved or Persian War raged.
- They have always known about AIDS, though they are unlikely to have had a polio vaccine shot.
- Cable, VCRs, compact discs, and answering machines have always been around.
- They have grown up with microwave popcorn and remote controls.

Teachers should consider what is personally meaningful to adolescents as they determine what content to teach. If a teacher decides that the evolving political structure in Germany is pertinent, this content can be made more relevant when compared to the more recent political struggles in China and Russia. Decisions about instructional delivery should similarly take into account the context of adolescents' social experiences. The information on the pages of a textbook cannot be altered fast enough to keep abreast of change in the world nor should adolescents' learning experiences be limited to what is written there.

Adolescent understanding is possible when teachers go beyond the "bits and pieces" of disconnected information. Specific dates of minor historical events or isolated facts that are not linked to broader issues, trends, or themes, for example, do not spark student interest or invite critical thought. Void of energy or dimension, this information is easily forgotten because it lacks the potential to connect with anything of relevance in adolescents' current or future lives. Absorbing this kind of information becomes more of a game of Trivial Pursuit than a process of thoughtful engagement with substantive knowledge.

Your Ideas

When adolescents encounter the "overarching mental images" that hold subject matter together, they can begin to develop an understanding of the important concepts, principles, and skills that shape the disciplines (Perkins 1992, 17). This kind of knowledge is "dynamic, intellectually intriguing, and personal," and understanding it can give a "sense of power" to adolescent learners (Tomlinson 1999, 31).

Arguably, curricular decisions need to consider national standards, state and local guidelines, and assessment measures. Teachers, however, can work strategically within these parameters to identify and select knowledge that lends itself to understanding (Wiggins and McTigue 1998). The process begins with deciding what knowledge is essential and enduring to the discipline. The following four questions based on those enunciated by Wiggins and McTigue (1998, 11) can guide teachers as they sort through the range of possibilities in a content area:

- Does the idea, topic, or process have enduring value beyond the classroom?
- Is the idea, topic, or process central to an understanding of the discipline?
- Is this an idea, topic, or process that is frequently confusing or less obvious?
- Does this idea, topic, or process have the potential to engage student interest?

Figure 5.1 is a visual representation of one teacher's thought processes during the planning of a social studies unit. The teacher's reasoning leads to some pertinent decisions about content. The broad learning goal encompasses the knowledge and skills the teacher deems important, and it is aligned with national curricular goals and standards. The teacher also spends considerable time identifying and prioritizing the knowledge and skills believed to be pertinent to historical understanding, such as the recognition of multiple and varying points of view.

Content Concepts

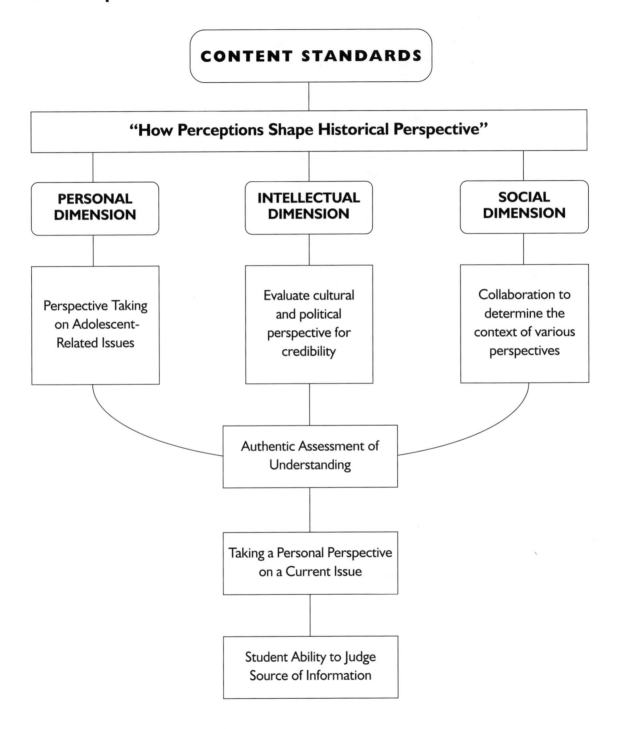

Figure 5.1

Once a teacher determines what is to be "covered," the next challenge is to plan learning experiences that will engage students with the content deemed necessary for deep understanding. These instructional opportunities will help the adolescents gain important knowledge, think from the perspective of a historian, and demonstrate their understanding. The ACT Model, "Teaching for Understanding," illustrates a learning experience that could be developed.

Your Ideas

Inquiry and Essential Questioning

In their book, *Understanding by Design*, Wiggins and McTigue (1998) distinguish between two types of questions that help students build an understanding of knowledge. These are essential questions, which are broad and more generalized, and topic- or lesson-specific questions. Essential questions deal with the more enduring ideas of a discipline. Topic-specific questions provoke thought about a particular piece of literature, work of art, scientific concept, mathematical problem, or historical event. They act as pathways to the more comprehensive essential questions (see Figure 5.2).

By engaging actively and collaboratively in the process of critical inquiry, teachers can help students broaden their thinking about the context for interpretation. They can create an opportunity for them to express their ideas and guide as they work for insight into the complex

Structuring Questions to Challenge Adolescent Thinking

Essential Question	Related Topic-Specific Questions
How does conflict shape history?	How did the bombing of Pearl Harbor change the dynamics of World War II?
How is interdependency reflected in environment?	What is the relationship among the strata of the rainforest?
How is symmetrical patterning apparent in nature?	What are the real-world implications of the Fibonacci sequence?
Should equity be prized at the expense of excellence?	Do you think it is fair that some of the ballet dancers in Vonnegut's (1968) "Harrison Bergeron" must wear weights on their legs?
How can nonconformity lead to creative expression?	What social, personal, and political factors influenced Dali's artistic style?

Figure 5.2

Teaching for Understanding: What's in a Perspective?

Adolescents may realize that historical accounts are based primarily on human interpretation. They frequently, however, believe that their own culture renders the true perspective and may be quick to deem alternate viewpoints as false. Perpetuated by history books and the media, this form of cultural stereotyping should be confronted. Teachers need to help students develop the critical thinking skills to determine the validity and credibility of varying perspectives. They also need to understand the social, cultural, and political context.

Content Understanding

To help adolescents to understand that human perspectives are shaped by complex historical, cultural, social, and political factors.

To develop the critical thinking skills to analyze and evaluate the credibility and authenticity of sources.

Essential Inquiry Questions

Why would the recorded accounts of an event in history differ?
How and why does propaganda originate? Is it ever justified?
How can the credibility of secondary sources be tested?
Are primary sources always reliable?

An Inquiry Task:

A Critical Analysis of Accounts of Events of Tiananmen Square, 1989

Guided Interaction

■ In preparation for the task, teachers can help adolescents practice perspective-taking through informal paired debates on various issues. The cultural, religious, and personal reasons that people have alternate viewpoints on issues can be discussed. Questions can be generated by students, such as those found on the Pro-Con chart on the following page. Students should be asked to support a perspective they would not ordinarily take.

Pro-Con Chart

	Pros	Cons
Should marijuana be legalized?		
Should animals be put at risk by the film industry?		
Is the death penalty ever justified?		
Should athletes be required to take a drug-screening test?		

- A video might be shown of the news coverage of the 1989 Tiananmen Square incident and the historical events that set a context for the event discussed (the Cultural Revolution, Mao's reign, the pro-democracy movement).
- Students should read conflicting excerpts from reports of the 1989 Tiananmen Square incident in Beijing, China, in Web sites such as Encarta Learning Zone's Encyclopedia online (http://encarta.msn.com/index) or Tiananmen: The Gate of Heavenly Peace, which contains several links to articles, essays, and book excerpts on the incident (http://www.nmis.org/Gate). Discrepancies should be noted and personal questions formulated.
- During an ensuing discussion, the teacher should probe about the historical events and conflicting political viewpoints among the Chinese people. Students can be expected to substantiate their responses with reference to source.

Task-Specific Questions
Is there an account that seems closer to the truth?
Are there similarities in any other accounts?
How can any account be justified?
Why would there be shock among Chinese officials at the protests?
How might the peoples' roles or age influence the perspective?
Does the date of the reporting make any difference?

Metacognitive Development and Assessment

- ■ Following the discussion about the Tiananmen Square accounts, the teacher should extend adolescents' thinking with reflection questions. These might include

  – Why do people see and interpret events differently?

  – How do personal emotions affect one's perspective?

  – Why is it important to consider historical and cultural context?

  – What is important to consider in the critical analysis of sources?

  – Do you think that what you read in the United States is always credible?

- ■ Teachers can promote transfer by using critical analysis skills in another context. Students could examine two local newspapers and contrast the language and perspectives of regional reporters or compare a large newspaper's angle on a story versus a small-town paper. Two book or play reviews might be read and research conducted on the reviewers. Stratified sampling surveys about political or environmental issues might be conducted and variations among respondents discussed. Polls across grade levels on school-related issues could be planned.

- ■ As a culminating assessment, students could write a persuasive letter (or editorial) to a pertinent source (newspaper or magazine) that reflects a personal perspective on a current issue. Evaluative criteria might include logical progression of reasoning, acknowledgment of alternate perspectives and their rationale, credible support for perspective, and coherence and organization.

Adapted from J. Chaffee (1997) *Thinking Critically,* 6th ed. Boston: Houghton Mifflin.

Cross-Disciplinary Applications

- ■ In art class students can be asked to take a painting of one artist and discuss how and why another from a different time period might approach the same subject.

- ■ A teacher might ask students to assume the roles of characters in different pieces of literature to discuss a modern-day issue, such as bioengineering or censorship. They would have to understand the setting context and values of the period as well as the characterization.

cultural and political conditions that shape perspective. Teachers can use questioning strategically to promote adolescent thinking and understanding.

Your Ideas

Questions, Questions, and More Questions

Over 2,000 years ago Socrates used questioning masterfully to guide student thinking about important knowledge. Rather than provide the answers, his style was to ask yet another question. The purpose of Socratic discussion, according to Paul and Binker (1995b), is to help students "develop and evaluate their thinking by making it explicit." The teacher's role is to "wonder aloud," to show interest in what students think, to respect what they say, and to encourage them to "slow their thinking down and elaborate on it" (1995b, 335). The teacher's role is to guide students as they arrive at their own answers. Socratic discussion can strengthen adolescents' abilities to reason logically about important knowledge.

Questioning can be used to help adolescents construct meaning from content and to think about knowledge in an extended, more refined manner (Marzano et al. 1992). By incorporating the language of thinking into questioning and by purposefully sequencing inquiry, teachers can also help to strengthen adolescents' metacognitive capacities (Beamon 1990, 1992-93, 1997). A long-term goal of strategic questioning is that adolescents will begin to use inquiry skills independently. The following self-evaluative questions can be useful to teachers as they engage adolescents in the process of inquiry, whether the focus is a novel, a historical interpretation, a problem, an experiment, or an art form (Beamon 1993, 1997):

- Do I ask higher-level questions that cause adolescents to think and reason?
- Do my questions connect with what students know and understand?
- Do I model my own (genuine) curiosity and interest in learning more?
- Do I withhold my viewpoint to encourage other ideas, yet delve when necessary into areas of misconception or narrow thinking?
- Do I expect students to present their viewpoints logically?
- Do I ask probing questions for clarification, substantiation, or extension?
- Do I set high standards for what is an acceptable response?
- Do I help students draw a connection from the immediate topic to a more relevant and abstract application?

*Your
Ideas*

- Do I expect students to listen respectfully to each other's views?
- Do my students feel comfortable enough to share their thinking?
- Do I allow adequate time for adolescents to think through or add to answers?

The "SAFE" Classification Model in Figure 5.3 was designed to help teachers formulate questions to challenge adolescent thinking on four cognitive levels (Beamon 1990, 1997). Questions on the first (**S**) level help adolescents "set up" a content knowledge base. These query for basic comprehension and answers are usually based on facts. Questions on the second (**A**) level are more analytical, however, and require adolescents to interpret contextual clues before answering. To respond to questions on the (**F**) level, adolescents must focus content in a direction different than originally presented. The fourth (**E**) level is a classification level that elicits students' evaluative thinking. Example questions illustrate possible content area applications.

Purposeful inquiry involves the strategic sequencing of cognitive questions. Teachers can order questions in a way that helps adolescents connect with knowledge and challenges them to think about it in more sophisticated ways. Through the conscious integration of cognitive questions and follow-up questions, teachers can sustain a high level of inquiry and prompt adolescents to think about and improve their thinking expression. The strategic sequencing of questions during a discussion of the Tiananmen Square accounts is illustrated in Figure 5.4. A few examples of follow-up questions are provided below.

- What is the reasoning for your answer?
- What is the basis for your conclusion?
- Is there an alternative way to look at the situation?
- What evidence supports your thinking?
- What else can you (or anyone) add to your (this) response?
- What contradiction do you recognize in your reasoning?
- What might be the consequences of this decision?
- What is an example of this situation in real life?
- How does this apply in another subject area?

The purposefully sequenced questioning in Figure 5.4 is an example of Socratic style. The teacher does not dominate the discussion but enters at strategic points. When an interjection is made, the teacher acknowledges students' responses or summarizes their ideas but does not give an opinion. Through purposeful questions that probe, ask for rationale, or redirect, the teacher is able to maintain the momentum of the discussion as the adolescents are challenged beyond surface-level or impulsive thinking toward more fully developed ideas. The teacher

Questioning To Challenge Adolescent Thinking: A "SAFE" Classification Model

Setting the Knowledge Base

Students are asked to remember facts, relate personal experiences, and make meaningful connections with new knowledge. These questions are literal, with fairly apparent answers.

What are the basic steps in this process?
What is the formula to find this function?
What are the events that led to this occurrence?
What other story was set in this location?
What in your own experience helps you relate to this character?
Who are other artists who used this style?

Analyzing the New Knowledge

These questions ask students to make inferences, to interpret information based on contextual clues, to compare or explain, and to see new relationships in the knowledge. These questions require an analysis of meaning, and answers are interpretive.

What relationship do you see among these number properties?
What can you infer about this character's motive?
How could we classify these genetic characteristics?
How does this problem-solving method compare to the other one?
How can you differentiate this perspective from the others?
Why is the historical event pivotal?

Focusing the New Knowledge

These questions encourage divergent thinking. Students are asked to make predictions, to hypothesize, to extend knowledge to a new context, or to focus it in new direction.

Based on what you've found, what hypothesis can you formulate?
If we change this angle, what will be the effect on the perimeter?
If the story took place in another time period, how might the ending change?
What is another way to view this decision?
If this composer could hear today's music, what might he say?

Evaluating the New Knowledge

These questions require students to evaluate, judge, appraise, critique, or give personal value to the new knowledge. They encourage personal reflection.

What is your perspective on the issue?
Which of the two methods worked more efficiently?
What criteria are you using to judge the value of the piece?
What argument could you present to verify your conclusion?
How can we determine the appropriateness of this decision?

Figure 5.3

Sequenced Questioning for Tiananmen Square Discussion

- What are your questions or observations after reading the accounts? [(**S**)*etting the knowledge level*]

- What do any of you know about the government of China or this particular protest? [(**S**)*etting the knowledge level*]

- How might your interpretation be different if you did not know that the student was in custody? [(**F**)*ocusing the knowledge in new direction*]

- Do you see any terms or statements that seem inflammatory or that make you think the account lacks complete credibility?

- What are other examples of emotional language? [**Follow-up** *for alternate ideas*]

- Why might the Chinese Chairman be compelled to justify the army's actions? [(**A**)*nalysis level*]

- Would you justify the Chairman's account? [(**E**)*valuative level*]

- Is there an account that seems closer to the truth? [(**A**)*nalysis level*]

- What evidence can you give for your thinking? [**Follow-up** *for substantiation*]

- Are there other reasons? [**Follow-up** *for more detail*]

- What do you think is the basis for these discrepancies? [**Follow-up** *for rationale*]

- What have you learned about the reporting of historical events? [(**E**)*valuative level for reflection on learning*]

- What is important to consider in the critical analysis of sources? [*Check for Understanding*]

- Do you think what you read in the United States is always credible? [(**E**)*valuative level*]

Figure 5.4

skillfully guides the discussion toward more thoughtful consideration of the enduring ideas of the discipline.

Putting Authenticity in the Learning Task

Well-developed authentic learning tasks for adolescents should meet several criteria (Marzano and Kendall 1991; McCombs 1993). These include the following:

- **Adolescent Directed.** The experience is structured to promote student choice, acceptance of responsibility, a sense of ownership, personal control, and metacognitive awareness. A language arts teacher could have teams of students design multimedia projects that featured the setting, characterization, plot, and theme of an adolescent novel. These projects can be used in the media center as interactive "booktalks" to entice their peers and promote school-wide reading.

*Your
Ideas*

- **Personally, Socially, and Content Relevant.** The experience is relevant to adolescents' interests and needs, and it extends to broader global issues such as human rights or environmental protection. It also carries importance within the discipline or subject area. A science class might prepare for an upcoming video conference with a NASA scientist on the impact of microgravity on gene expression in order to write a position paper on government spending in space.

- **Knowledge Intensive.** The experience requires adolescents to know the subject matter thoroughly and meaningfully. It also prompts them to view knowledge from multiple perspectives and to use content across disciplines. A social studies class could learn about the complexity of local government by simulating a town meeting of parents, students, teachers, officials, and business persons to debate the construction of a waterslide on property adjacent to a middle school. The students could vote and project future consequences.

- **Complex and Cognitively Compelling.** The experience necessitates higher-order thinking through inquiry, data collection and analysis, decision making, and reflective mental processing. A variety of reasoning processes is activated as adolescents question, investigate, experiment, compare, classify, substantiate, and problem solve. A math class might analyze how many hamburgers were eaten in their city by gathering and comparing data from the Web sites of the National Beef Council and the U.S. Census Bureau.

- **Product Oriented.** The experience directs adolescents toward a final product or performance that is appropriate and accommodates learning preference. These might include panel discussion, a Web-based project, a videotaped documentary, a written or oral report, or a dramatic presentation. A computer graphics class could collaborate with the local chamber of commerce in the design for a new logo that would capture and commemorate the county's direction for the 21st century.

- **Collaborative.** The task invites cooperation and collaborative engagement. A Spanish class can produce language demonstration videos based on popular cultural music and clothing adver-

*Your
Ideas*

tisements for ESL students at a neighboring elementary school to strengthen language skills.

- **Time Intensive.** The experience is generally long-term compared to more traditional instructional tasks. Through the use of electronic discussion, students might conduct a study of the language use and specialized vocabulary of selected groups in the community.

Authentic learning experiences do more than merely involve adolescents in fun activities. Students work together to design products or to engage in performances that challenge them to build and think about knowledge in a context that resembles a real-life experience. The products, such as the book talks, millennium logos, and instructional videotapes in the above examples, are often contributions to the school and local community. These experiences frequently enable adolescents to consider the varying viewpoints of people involved in a realistic problem. To prepare for these tasks, students may need to gather data and discuss different perspectives on complex issues. To produce them, they need a good knowledge of content. In authentic learning experiences, adolescents are motivated and self-directed, and they gain a better understanding of the broader ideas of the discipline.

Perhaps the strongest illustration of authentic learning experiences is problem-based learning (PBL). The knowledge gained through problem-based learning extends beyond the factual to a higher conceptual level. This instructional method is the topic of the next section.

Building Knowledge Collaboratively

In his book, *Teaching for Thoughtfulness*, John Barell proposed problem-based learning (PBL) as an instructional approach that challenges students "to engage in significant, authentic, and meaningful intellectual work" that places them in "the more active role of taking greater control of their own learning" (1995, 120). A professor and noted author in thinking development at Montclair State University, Barell wrote that students need multiple opportunities and sufficient time to think productively about major ideas, concepts, and principles. He made the plea that ideas be the "main characters" of learning (1995, 134). He cautioned against the memorization of textbook explanations and abstract applications, and promoted learning experiences that confront students with complex situations that must be thought about and resolved through collaborative, knowledge-building effort. Barell explained that these situations are the ones that prime students for the complex problem solving of real life.

As in actual situations, the PBL problems are "ill-structured" and require adolescents, as problem solvers, to seek out essential missing information (called learning issues). Students pool their knowledge for a final product or resolution. These problems invite questioning, promote purposeful collaboration among adolescents, teachers, and others, and may alter in focus as information is gathered. The emphasis is placed on the students' ability to access pertinent and multiple sources, and to synthesize data to address and solve the problem (Gallagher 1997). In most cases, problem-based situations challenge adolescents to examine information from a variety of disciplinary viewpoints, and often problems include real-life ethical issues. The skills for critical thinking are developed through collaborative inquiry and knowledge building, and adolescents assume much responsibility over their learning. The ACT Model in the "Problem-Based Learning (PBL) Application" provides an example.

*Your
Ideas*

A Problem-Based Learning (PBL) Application: Is This a Question of Censorship?

Problem-based learning confronts adolescents with loosely-structured problems that could realistically occur in their own experience. Students hypothesize about missing information, determine resources and strategies for data collection, and generate thoughtful solutions. Much choice and responsibility are afforded to the adolescents, although the teacher plays a strategic role as facilitator and guide during the inquiry process.

Content Understanding

To help adolescents explore the issue of censorship and the school's role related to Internet restriction and to promote skills for problem solving and inquiry.

Strategies for Inquiry

■ The teacher can set the background by having students respond in their journals and exchange ideas about the following broad questions before presenting the problem:

Do schools have a right to place restrictions on what students read or view?

Why do people often disagree about what should be restricted?

When does censorship infringe on human rights?

The Inquiry Problem

You are excited that finally all classrooms and labs in the school system have been wired for Internet access, and Web-based resources are now available. Your teacher comes in one morning, however, with the news that several parents have petitioned the school board asking that Internet use be halted. An open forum is scheduled for next month's meeting.

Memo

To: Hooverville Teachers

From: The Supertindent

Subject: Internet Use in Classrooms

Parents of students in the system have expressed considerable concerns about the use of the Internet in classrooms and have petitioned that access be restricted. The matter will be discussed at the next School Board meeting. Until then, all Internet use should be halted.

Guided Interaction

■ Guiding questions can be posed to help students define the problem and determine known and missing information. These might include the following:

What is the challenge presented to us?

What do we think we know to resolve this situation?

How and where might be find the information we need?

■ Teachers should help adolescents develop a research plan and map out strategies. Sources might include other school systems with Internet policies, K–12 teachers who use Web-based instruction, and other students and parents. Data can be collected through interviews, surveys, or Web sites. Teachers will also need to supervise as students organize for research.

■ Students will need the teacher's guidance further during a discussion of initial findings:

Are people's opinions biased? Realistic? Why or why not?

Are other plans working? Is there any flexibility for different age groups? Should there be?

■ Later in the process, the teacher should help determine a format for organizing and presenting findings—written plan, report, or oral presentation.

Metacognitive Development and Assessment

■ Teachers can help students to monitor progress as teams work on fact finding and analysis. Assessment questions might include, How well are you doing? Do you need to change strategy? Are you finding what you need? Is it making sense?

■ Collaboration among teacher and adolescents to set criteria for the final product is important.

■ Criteria could include a feasibility of suggestions, consideration for varying ages, attempt to address needs, or interest of persons involved. Assessment should also be based on group and individual contribution.

■ If feasible, teachers should arrange a format for presentation or sharing that includes pertinent people involved in the research who can provide evaluative feedback.

■ Time will need to be scheduled for follow-up reflection: How well did we do? Were we cooperative? What have we learned about ourselves? About others? What will we do differently next time? Why? What strategies worked? Transfer can be promoted by discussing application of problem-solving strategies in other realistic situations.

Cross-Disciplinary Applications

■ An English teacher might present students with a modern-day problem scenario that reflects a novel's dilemma, such as an instance prejudice, prior to reading *To Kill A Mockingbird* or *The Adventures of Huckleberry Finn*; civil rights and censorship, prior to *Fahrenheit 451* or *The Crucible*; and biogenetics, prior to reading *Brave New World*.

■ Other problem-based scenarios can be shaped around ethical issues in various content areas or that apply the skills of the discipline. Inquiry into the status of rain forest depletion makes use of mathematical skills to analyze data from online sources. Language arts skills are incorporated by having students write perspective papers or debate positions.

Barell (1995) and other educators, including Stepien and Gallagher (1997) and Schoenfeld (1985) and Torpa and Saje (1998), have supported problem-based learning for reasons that are pertinent to students' personal, social, and intellectual development. These points summarize the value of this methodology for adolescent learners:

Your Ideas

1. Problem situations are motivational because they initially perplex, intrigue, and catch adolescents' interest.
2. Problem-based learning requires adolescents to gather relevant information from a variety of sources and to consider and role play multiple perspectives.
3. Well-designed problems encompass important cross-curricular concepts that are historically "timeless" and currently pertinent.
4. Adolescents can become more enlightened in their personal perceptions of others' viewpoints and cultural orientation and more ethical in their value formation.
5. The inquiry process supports the role of the teacher as cognitive coach and the adolescent as the apprentice who gains knowledge and becomes independent.
6. Adolescents use information in a meaningful way and are better able to retain the content and apply the problem-solving strategies in new situations.
7. The process promotes reflection and adolescent metacognitive development.

Group Work Really Can Work

Much emphasis has been placed throughout the book on the impact of shared cognition, distributed intelligence, and collaborative communities of learners, yet as any teacher of adolescents knows: Putting a group of teenagers together in a group is risky. As social as adolescents naturally are, they do not as naturally have the social and personal skills to work together in a group toward a common academic goal. The research, however, is clear. For students at any age, cooperative learning promotes positive self-concept, academic achievement, critical thinking, peer relationship, social behavior, and motivation to learn (Johnson 1979; Johnson et al. 1981; Johnson and Johnson 1983; 1989). Interactive group work, implemented effectively, can benefit adolescents socially, personally, and intellectually.

A plethora of strategies, structures, and models are currently available to guide teachers as they plan for collaborative learning (Bellanca and Fogarty 1991; Johnson and Johnson 1983; Kagan 1990;

Your Ideas

Slavin 1980; Sharan and Sharan 1976). Teachers accordingly need to be selective as to when, why, and how they incorporate peer grouping into instruction. In simple terms, group work needs to be purposeful.

If a teacher wants to promote group inquiry into broad questions, such as Is there a relationship between global warming and natural disasters? or How has the computer impacted the business market economy?, for example, Sharan and Sharan's (1976) Group Investigation Model might be used. Through a similar method, Kagan's (1990) Jigsaw structure, adolescents share the responsibility for a specific section of the information under study. Other structured inquiry models include problem- and project-based learning. In each of these models, adolescents follow a series of steps and are assigned specific responsibilities. Assessment is usually both individual and collaborative through a final group product.

Simpler cooperative learning structures, such as think-pair-share or numbered heads together (Kagan 1990), can be used flexibly for different purposes within daily instruction. At the beginning of a lesson, for example, students can recall what they know about a topic or concept, and share with a partner. Pairs of students can join other sets of two to compare hypotheses or procedures (Bellanca and Fogarty 1991). For the "numbered heads together structure," each student in a small group has a number. Periodically during a lesson, the teacher may ask the small group to discuss a new concept; however, specific questions are asked using a random number call. The student with the number three might be asked to respond in one group, for example, and his or her counterpart in another group might be asked to elaborate, explain, or give an alternate answer. Figure 5.5 gives several ideas for purposeful collaborative activity based on the work of Daniels and Bizer (1998) and Fogarty and Bellanca (1995).

For collaborative grouping, simple or formal, to work well, "solid procedures for keeping groups productive" should be in place (Daniels and Bizar 1998, 60):

> If a teacher is going to turn kids loose in several simultaneously-meeting groups, he by definition can not be managing and guiding everyone at once, which means the groups' activities must have enough inherent structure to operate autonomously, to remain engaging, on-task, and relevant.

Additionally, adolescents need to be taught the skills for interpersonal interaction and the specific strategies for productive collaboration. They also need to know if, when, and how well they demonstrate the expected behaviors in order to improve. A few guiding questions might be useful as teachers make decisions about group work (Marcus and McDonald 1990):

1. Where is the challenge? To feel a sense of concerted purpose, adolescents need to be engaged in significant activity that stimulates their thinking, such as a problem to solve, a decision to make, a debate to construct, or a project to create. They also need help with skills, including decision-making, problem solving, persuasion, or consensus building.

2. Where is the interdependence? Adolescents need to be involved in a joint effort that requires the interaction of all members. Are they expected to achieve a goal or product, such as a decision, solution, project, or presentation? Is the group involvement purposeful and dependent on teamwork and shared cooperation?

3. Where is the accountability? In cooperative activities, adolescents need to feel individually responsible for personal contribution. Is there an assigned role, a personal response, an individual quiz, a contract, or a self/group evaluation form?

4. Where is the interpersonal development? Group interaction depends on and should extend adolescents' social skills. Dispositions, including respect for others' opinions, consensus building, contribution of ideas, or perspective seeking should be targeted and evaluated.

5. Where is the reflection? Accompanying group interaction should be a time to think back over and "debrief" about the process, to self-evaluate, and to assess the contributions of members of the group, socially and academically. The final product should be evaluated according to expected criteria.

Group work can be meaningful for adolescent learning if it is planned well and if teachers have instilled in students the skills and dispositions for purposeful collaboration. Working together effectively is not easy. Instruction, practice and feedback are prerequisites, and the teacher's interactive role is essential. Structure and accountability must be apparent through specific guidelines for tasks, communicated expectations for behavior and demonstration, and organized procedures for evaluation and reflection. Adolescents enjoy the opportunity to work together to learn, yet they need to know when they are meeting expected learning standards, both academic and behavioral. Ongoing assessment that supplies constructive feedback can help adolescents direct the activity of their learning productively and positively manage their actions toward one another.

Your Ideas

Nothing's Simple

As with young Jonas in *The Giver* (Lowry 1993), who begins to realize the complexities, the subtleties, and the magnificence of a world dis-

Using Group Work Purposefully

When Discussion Is Needed

- Literature Circles—Student-led discussion groups that meet regularly to talk about books or other literary works.

- Classroom Workshops—From literacy to mathematics, students go through a set schedule of mini-lessons, work time interaction, feedback and sharing.

- Focus Groups—Each group is given a facet of a problem or an element of a piece of literature. Topics can also be selected according to interests. A set of thought questions helps to guide this seminar-modeled discussion.

Mainly For Partners

- Dialogue Journals—Pairs of students write and exchange "conversations" on a regular basis about content, such as a story, a scientific concept, or an historical event.

- Paired for Action—Students are paired and given interlocking assignments that require joint activity for experimentation, observation, or reading. Partners can also be used to clarify ideas about concepts, for "think alouds" during problem solving, for "think-pair-share" dyads, or to "punctuate" a lecture, reading, or film, as in "turn to your partner and share."

Grouped for Inquiry

- Student Survey Teams—Adolescents choose a social issue, such as freedom of speech, gun control, drug control and prejudice, design and send surveys to a targeted population, analyze results, exhibit findings, and respond personally to the issue through writing and discussion.

- Group Investigation Models—A jigsaw method used for more sophisticated inquiry. Each student is responsible for a part of information that must be reassembled or synthesized to complete the whole "puzzle."

- Problem-Based Learning (PBL)—Students solve ill-structured problems or research problem situations by posing questions, gathering information, analyzing results, and often presenting findings in a creative way.

- WebQuests—Structured project-based inquiry into a real-world problem with research mainly through Web sites. Final products are often posted on the Web.

Figure 5.5

closed through knowledge, understanding can free the adolescents' minds from the limitation of egocentric perspectives and naïve perceptions. Also, as with Jonas, the door to understanding opens into a world of paradox, where all is not what it might appear or seem, and nothing is simple. Parker Palmer (1999) wrote that true insight comes with the acquired capacity "to hold paradoxes together"—to recognize and integrate the apparent contradictions that give life its complexity (1999, 65). As Gardner similarly observed, "There is no need to look for the single, privileged approach to important concepts, for none exists . . . . But the purpose of education is not to provide ultimate answers; it is to enhance one's sense of understanding without dashing one's sense of mystery and wonder" (1999, 185).

Your Ideas

Theodore R. and Nancy F. Sizer of the Coalition of Essential Schools summarized this challenge well (1999, 103):

> Schools exist to change young people. They should be different— better—for their experience there. They should know some important things, they should know how to learn additional important things, they should be in the habit of wanting to learn such important things. They should have a reasoned, but individual point of view. They should be judicious, aware of the complexity of the world. They should be thoughtful, respectful of thought and of ideas which are the furniture of thought.

Teaching for understanding liberates adolescents' minds in a way that inspires active and continuous intellectual inquiry and self-discovery.

ACTing
on the Adolescent-Centered Learning
Principles Discussed in Chapter 5

Principle	*How I can put it into practice*
❏ Develop and use instructional approaches that promote adolescent understanding through active inquiry, purposeful collaboration, and supportive technology.	
❏ View assessment as ongoing and integral to learning, as an opportunity for students to demonstrate understanding.	
❏ Free adolescent minds from the limitations of egocentric perspectives and naïve perceptions so that they can be inspired to active and continuous intellectual inquiry and self discovery.	
❏ Facilitate cognitive connection by allowing students to see the nuances and patterns and to relate these ideas and concepts meaningfully.	
❏ Show students multiple pathways to examine knowledge, to construct personal meaning, and to know themselves more fully.	

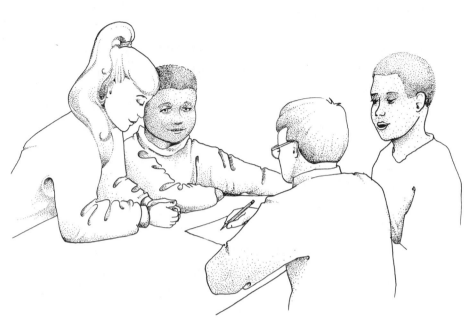

Content as a Way of Thinking

Shaping Thinking

Adolescents need multiple pathways to examine knowledge, to construct personal meaning, and to know themselves more fully. Within each content area is a potential for relevance, extension, and impact on how adolescents view themselves, the world, and their place in it. Central to each content area is the process of inquiry. The challenge to teachers is not to deliver an inert body of knowledge but to immerse young people in a richness of content and to guide them as they actively grapple, explore, collaborate, and learn. Ultimately, these students will have to integrate the experiences of schooling into a personal philosophy of living and interacting.

The following sections explore the unique domains of several disciplinary areas in terms of their encompassing ideas and their patterns of thinking. The instructional examples are designed specifically to facilitate adolescent learning and to promote students' social, personal, and intellectual development.

*Your
Ideas*

A different ACT is provided to illustrate adolescent learning in five content areas. In mathematics, the instructional emphasis is on the development of qualitative reasoning skills. In social studies, adolescents delve into critical issues that form the potential for civic action. Project-based inquiry is the format to construct scientific understanding and Socratic questioning challenges adolescents to consider literary viewpoints. In fine arts students assume an active role in learning management and exhibition. The value of a solid disciplinary understanding lies in the potential for the collective impact of knowledge on adolescents' future experiences.

Mathematics

The example in the ACT, "Reasoning Through Mathematics," is based on a research study (Schoen et al. 1999) that compared the reasoning ability of adolescents taught mathematics in a traditional way with another group taught through guided inquiry and authentic problem-solving. The latter group were more inclined to assess mathematical problems holistically versus just doing the calculation, to use graphing calculators, to verbalize and reflect on their thinking processes, and to see the connection between an abstract formula and what it represented in real life.

Mathematics is more than being able to use computational skill, though knowing how to calculate is important. Competence in mathematics is being able to use computational skills to reason, solve problems, test conjectures, and represent data in meaningful ways. With a wealth of information available on the Internet, the challenge to adolescents is not to obtain facts but to make sense of what they find. Ultimately, the goal of mathematics is to help students use the acquired skills purposefully in their own lives.

Reasoning Through Mathematics: "Head Math" Beware!

Adolescents need assistance as they reason through mathematical problems. Effective mathematics instruction requires teachers to model, guide, and give appropriate feedback, or suitable scaffolding, to ensure that they reason accurately. They also need assistance in connecting mathematical abstractions to real life applications.

Content Goals

To help adolescents use mathematical reasoning to solve problems dealing with quadratic equations and relationships among speed, height, and scientific phenomenon.

Strategies for Inquiry

The Inquiry Problem: The Bulldogs' pitcher and center fielder were standing together near the pitcher's mound during pre-game warm-up. The pitcher threw the baseball straight up with a velocity of 125 feet per second for the center fielder to catch. The height (h) of the ball after seconds (t) is represented by $h = -16t2 + 125t$.

Inquiry Questions

    a. What assumption might be made about the pattern of the time-height relationship on a graph?

    b. What would you predict to be the height of the baseball after four seconds?

    c. Write an equation whose solution is the number of seconds after the baseball is thrown that is 158 feet above the ground. Solve the equation, check it, and write the rationale for your strategy.

Guided Interaction

    ■ The teacher should keep adolescents from jumping to quick solutions that merely "plug in" the formula. They need to be encouraged to visualize what the formula means. Guiding questions might include

        – What is the problem asking us?

- How do you think the relationship would appear on a graph? What can you visualize?

- If we were to plot time along the horizontal axis and height on the vertical, what might the pattern be?

- What would the figure resemble?

■ Students should be asked to make and check assumptions on graphing calculators. Other questions might include,

- What might be faulty about your reasoning?

- What do you know about velocity, acceleration, and the force of gravity?

■ Students can work parts b and c in pairs, and then be asked to explain their rationale.

Metacognitive Development and Assessment

■ When the problems have been solved, teacher should ask these reflection questions:

- What thinking strategies did you use to solve this problem?

- How did trying to visualize the scenario help with your reasoning?

- What is the disadvantage of hasty thinking?

- How did our reasoning together help you understand the formula better?

- How did the graphing calculators help you as a "thinking tool"?

- What are some other real world examples that reflect the same concept?

- How would the formula change if the ball game took place on Mars?

■ A homework assessment could be an independent problem that applies mathematical reasoning to a related authentic situation, as follows:

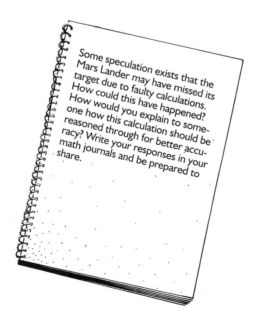

Some speculation exists that the Mars Lander may have missed its target due to faulty calculations. How could this have happened? How would you explain to someone how this calculation should be reasoned through for better accuracy? Write your responses in your math journals and be prepared to share.

Connecting adolescent mathematical learning to what is real is easier today through technology. Statistics can be accessed from Web sites for analysis and display in graphs and spreadsheets. Digital processing creates an instant visualization of 3-D geometrical images, such as a satellite picture of the Earth for the study of pi. Mathematical instruction that involves realistic inquiry also enables adolescents to make connections across other disciplines and with real experiences (Drier et al. 1999). The following Web sites provide a variety of real-world data that can be accessed, displayed through spreadsheets, calculated, and analyzed.

Your Ideas

Useful Web Sites for Real-World Data for Mathematics and Problem Solving

- National Geophysical Data Center
  (http://www.ngdc.noaa.gov)
- National Oceanic and Atmospheric Administration
  (http://www.noaa.gov),
- Prevention Web site
  The Center for Disease Control
  (http://www.cdc.gov)
- National Center for Health Statistics Web site
  (http://www.cdc.gov/nchs)
- InvestSmart
  (http://library.thinkquest.org/10326)

Social Studies

Teaching social studies effectively ultimately involves active engagement with important knowledge through guided inquiry, interactive discourse, and thoughtful reflection. The teacher's role is not to tell, but to model the timeless and ongoing quest to understand people and their relationships, roles, and responsibilities as participants in a global society. Student ownership, challenge, choice, variety, technology, social interaction, community connections, real-world tasks, and authentic assessment are what make a lesson compelling and successful. Although an independent performance is expected, students collaborate about ideas and resources, and assist each other with the technology applications.

Making an Issue
of Social Studies:
Taking Civic Action

For social studies to be meaningful to adolescents, it should be taught through important ideas and enduring questions. Because it encompasses a variety of disciplines, including history, economics, civics, sociology, anthropology, culture, and geography, it also needs to connect across content, time, and space. Social studies understanding further involves an awareness of the values, beliefs, and attitudes that shape personal and human interaction. By developing and promoting a personal perspective under a teacher's guidance, adolescents are more likely to act independently with ethical and civic-minded responsibility.

Content Understanding

To help adolescents

■ conceptualize that critical issues have a context often defined by varying personal beliefs and value systems;

■ be able to engage in reflective social inquiry;

■ understand that the consequences of their choices and actions impact themselves and others; and

■ assume responsibility for ethical civic action as citizens in a global community.

Strategies for Inquiry

The Task: Over the next two months you are going to develop a position on a critical issue that faces us in this new century. Your task is to assemble a collection of materials that an activist on the issue might want to have. You will use the format of an electronic portfolio. Suggested categories for modern-day issues include

individual beliefs/majority rule   cultural diversity/cultural assimilation

national security/individual freedom   individual rights/public safety

national—state/community control   community progress/individual liberties

global enterprise/national interests   worker security/employer rights

Guided Interaction

Guiding Questions on Sample Issues

■ When does world security take priority over domestic interests? When should it?

Consider understanding American involvement in global concerns, such as the AIDS epidemic in sub-Saharan Africa, the turmoil in Chechnya, world hunger, and natural disasters such as the flooding devastation in Turkey.

■ When does national power infringe on local control or individual rights? When should it?

Topics include censorship, prayer in schools, dress codes, cultural diversity, drug testing, cancer treatments, gun control, violence prevention, life choice, and media management.

■ When does progress conflict with cultural or environmental protection? When should it?

Think about struggles among environmentalists, private citizens, and economists, such as rain forest destruction, pollution of air and streams, logging in natural forests, endangered species, and technological expansion.

■ What should be the "new frontier" of the new millennium?

Shape perspectives on the priority for global resources, such as medicine, space, bioengineering, ocean harvesting, and global relationship.

Metacognitive Development and Assessment

■ The portfolio provides an excellent metacognitive tool to help as students set goals, gauge progress, and stay active in their evaluation process. An exhibition day can enable parents and others involved to participate, and final projects, such as CDs with videoclips and "published" Web pages, can be shared with parent organizations, community groups, and other schools. The projects can also be used in adolescents' professional portfolios after graduation. See criteria in Figure 6.1.

Portfolio Components

____**A Creative Title**

____**A Table of Contents with Pagination**

____**A Formal Opening (200 words)**

> Describe your issue and your rationale for its selection.
> Provide an overview for what you project to accomplish in this portfolio.

____**Research**

> The critique of at least two annotated articles (online or print) supporting your position.
> The critique of at least two annotated articles (online or print) challenging your position.
> The script of an interview (face-to-face, phone, or online) with at least one expert on your issue.

____ **Legal Implications**

> An explanation of current local, state, and federal laws or procedures pertaining to your issue

____**Promotional Pieces (Minimum of 3)**

> An original slogan, bumper sticker or political cartoon designed with graphic software.
> A twenty-line jingle to be shared with the class through hypermedia software.
> A tri-fold pamphlet of professional quality that highlights the pros and cons of the issue.
> A printed editorial for a newspaper that supports your stance.
> A videotaped public service announcement that promotes your issue.

____**Civic Action Grant Proposal**

> Formulate a project to be enacted on behalf of the issue and write a proposal for supportive funding.
> Include a cover letter written on behalf of the issue.
> Prepare a three to five minute hypermedia presentation for the class.

____**A Formal Closing (500 words)**

> Summarize findings, justify your position, and suggest future activities that will further your cause.

____**Bibliography (at least 5 sources consulted)**

____**Supporting Illustrations and Graphics**

Figure 6.1

Science

Your Ideas

Good science instruction for adolescents means giving them time to explore, to observe, to make mistakes, to build and collect things, to calibrate instruments, to construct models, to investigate, to wrestle with the unfamiliar, and to come to "see the advantage of thinking differently" (Nelson 1999, 16). How can you design a paper airplane to go the maximum distance or the fastest speed or illustrate the principles of aeronautics? More than a body of knowledge or set of answers, science is a way of thinking about the world (Adams and Hamm 1999). This constructivist approach promotes active and collaborative inquiry as the basis for adolescent learning. Adolescents are full of wonder, and science is a good way to discover answers that lead to more questions.

The example in the ACT, "Inquiry into Science," gives ideas for project-based learning at the middle school level that capitalizes on the extensive online resources of NASA. A jigsaw would be useful to structure the group inquiry, and student roles could be assigned by interests or to differentiate the tasks for different ability levels. The opportunities for authentic collaboration and performance assessment are limitless.

Project-based learning promotes scientific understanding through collaboration and inquiry. Topics can range from those related to space exploration, nuclear safety, and energy control to wetland ecology, environmental science, waste management, and endangered species. Adolescents attain a good knowledge of scientific principles and apply valuable problem solving skills in an authentic context.

Inquiry into Science: Lost in Space?

Project-based learning, particularly when enhanced by technology, can provide an excellent vehicle for inquiry into complex content. Since 1964 when the Mariner 4 made its first flyby of the "red planet," NASA had been involved in an ongoing program of Mars exploration. The following inquiry challenge is based on the fate and status of the $164 million Polar Lander project.

Content Understanding

To help adolescents understand the geology and climate conditions that sustain life and the aerodynamics of space travel.

Strategies for Inquiry

The Challenge:

■ A small tape recorder might play the following message:

The loss of communication with the Mars Polar Lander has prompted NASA to assemble a team of scientists to investigate the project's failure. Your mission, should you decide to take it, is to plan for a successful follow-up landing. Projected launch date: June 1, 2001.

Guided Interaction

■ Student roles for the inquiry can be modeled after the real Mars Lander team, after scientists with varying expertise, such as geologists, astronomers, biologists, or by mission tasks, such as the climate investigators, the design team, the project overseer, mission controllers.

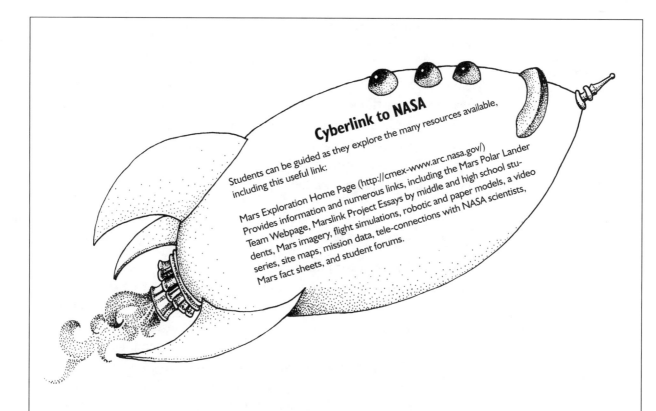

Cyberlink to NASA

Students can be guided as they explore the many resources available, including this useful link:

Mars Exploration Home Page (http://cmex-www.arc.nasa.gov/) Provides information and numerous links, including the Mars Polar Lander Team Webpage, Marslink Project Essays by middle and high school students, Mars imagery, flight simulations, robotic and paper models, a video series, site maps, mission data, tele-connections with NASA scientists, Mars fact sheets, and student forums.

Metacognitive Development and Assessment

- Ongoing assessment can include learning logs, experiments, letters, essays, creative and reflective writing, simulations, virtual site visits, forum discussion, maps and computer designs, data analyses, graphs, readings, and interviews.

- Findings could be presented to a Congressional committee, "published" on a NASA-linked Web page or in a flight mission manual (electronic or print), or shared through an interactive online "summit" with other student teams.

Your Ideas

What are the social, cognitive, and emotional benefits of inquiry-oriented science instruction for today's adolescents? They share the responsibility for thinking and doing. They are motivated to explore relevant and interesting situations and challenged to construct scientific meaning. Their thinking is stimulated and reasoning skills are honed. They interact in a social and realistic community of practice where they have the resources that support their learning. Scientific inquiry in the real world involves human exploration and making sense from discovery that is often unanticipated.

Language Arts

Adolescents may never publish poetry or novels or short stories. They should, however, gain a sense of the power of the written word to convey feeling and an author's perspective. Teachers can help students relate to literature and learn to communicate their ideas more effectively by creating numerous opportunities for them to think from the vantage of another. Helping adolescents understand the power of words to convey feeling and perspective has a direct implication on their personal and interpersonal development. Ultimately, this knowledge can help adolescents better understand themselves and their own view of the world. The following ACT Model, "Seminar in Session" illustrates an instructional method that can help facilitate this understanding.

Through a teacher's strategic questioning, adolescents are challenged to think about literature and to articulate their ideas. Relevant and emotionally-engaging discussion can tap and help shape and broaden student's perspectives as learners.

Seminar in Session: Living in a World of Sameness

The guided discussion of a popular novel can help adolescents relate to the emotional, social and intellectual development of a character their own age. A teacher's questions can help students "step" into the fictional role and, in turn, learn more about their own feelings and ideas. The Newbery Medal novels provide a rich source for interpretive inquiry into issues that interest adolescents.

Content Understanding

To help adolescents understand the multiple meanings and interpretations of text and to use the language effectively for a designated purpose and audience.

Strategies for Inquiry

An Inquiry-Based Seminar of the novel, *The Giver,* by Lois Lowry (1994)
Key questions for interpretation:

■ What would it be like to live in a world with no feeling or color or pain?

■ How can you reconcile a society of Sameness with human choice, integrity, and intellect?

Guided Interaction

■ A teacher might begin the seminar with an analysis-level question, such as
Why was Jonas perplexed when he noticed something different about Fiona's hair?

■ Depending on students' responses, other questions might probe, refocus, guide, or extend thinking, such as

– Why was this so disturbing to Jonas?

– How does knowing there is an Elsewhere make it worse to live in a society of Sameness?

– What is the rationale for the Sameness?

– Does intelligence might have anything to do with Jonas' discontent?

Metacognitive Development and Assessment

■ Other questions might enable students to extend the meaning of a text into their own lives, such as

– What is the "downside" of living in a world with no options?

– Why might the right of choice be important to human beings?

– What causes people pain in their lives?

– Would you give up choice and color to not have any pain?

– Can you think of instances in our lives when we choose to have no choice?

■ As an extension students could be given a writing prompt, such as: The Receiver continues to worry about Jonas. Write a letter back to his mentor that describes what happens in the youngster's life after the novel ends. Indicate if he is happy and why.

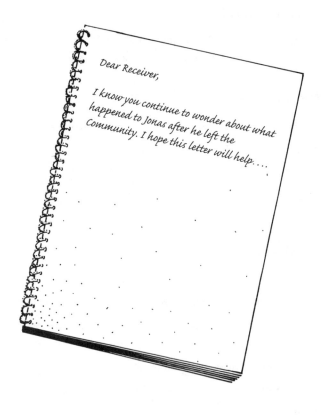

Dear Receiver,

I know you continue to wonder about what happened to Jonas after he left the Community. I hope this letter will help. . . .

Fine Arts

The potential of art to connect with adolescents' lives is recognized increasingly in schools across the country. No longer limited to those with special talents, art has become a vehicle for perspective taking, problem solving, and connection with other subject areas. Art studies revolve around local painters who have written books about their technique. Art teachers have teamed with English teachers to link pieces of literature and paintings that correspond in content and style. This potential to promote self-regulated learning in adolescent learners is also evident in the theatre arts and music (Mann 1998). Adolescents participate in mentoring and community internships by assuming year-long positions as company manager, costume coordinator, sound and light coordinators, and box office managers for local theaters.

The ACT Model, "Student-Directed Learning and Exhibition," is an example of an extensive project that served as a culminating performance assessment for an upper level art class. Adolescents prepared for this major project by painting seascapes and still life and by learning through perspective drawing, mixed media, collage, pen and ink, sculpture, and print making. The teacher's feedback during these preliminary exercises helped students gain the skills and confidence for the more complex task.

Art instruction can meet the emotional, intellectual, and social needs of adolescent learners. An understanding of technique, style, and context can serve as a springboard for creativity and personal expression as students gain knowledge and an appreciation for art and its value in their lives.

Your Ideas

Student-Directed Learning and Exhibition: The Study of an Artist

Adolescents need guidance as they acquire the self-management skills to direct their own learning, yet ultimately they should be given the freedom and responsibility to carry out a project independently. This in-depth artist study is an example. Students might choose Matisse, Cezanne, Dali, Warhol, Monet, and Van Gogh, although they can be encouraged to explore others, such as the 17th Century Dutch painter Vermeer. The culminating performance assessment provides an exhibition format that enables adolescents to "shine" before their peers.

Content Understanding

To enable adolescents to demonstrate an in-depth understanding of the style of a chosen artist.

The Inquiry-Based Research

Choose and research an artist of your choice. Your final products must include

1. a research paper about the artist and his or her unique style (the final exam grade);
2. a small copy of a specific work of the artist (to study technique and medium);
3. a large original work that emulated the artist's style in modern day context; and
4. a presentation before the class about the artist, using your art work as visuals.

Guided Interaction

■ The teacher should establish expectations for the project and monitor as students proceed through the four phases. Frequent checkpoints and feedback are critical.

Metacognitive Development and Assessment

■ Teachers should require students to keep ongoing journals for the project in order to reflect about their sketches and products.

■ The final research paper should be carefully assessed for grammar, spelling, and format. A sample rubric can be seen in Figure 6.2.

Research Paper Rubric

Content	Strong (10 pts)	Average (8-9 pts)	Weak (7pts)
1. Contains an interesting and informative introduction with stated topic or paper thesis			
2. Develops the thesis thoroughly; supporting information is accurate and appropriate			
3. Contains a conclusion that logically summarizes ideas presented about the topic			
4. Uses and properly references a variety of sources			
Form			
1. Includes a well-developed introduction, body, and conclusion that demonstrate proper, effective paragraphing			
2. Uses appropriate transitional words and phrases between sentences and paragraphs and includes a variety of sentence structures			
3. Demonstrates correct use of parenthetical documentation			
4. Uses correct bibliographical entries and format on reference page			
Usage, Mechanics, and Spelling			
1. Errors in grammar and usage: 0-1, strong; 2-4, average; more than 4, weak			
2. Develops the thesis thoroughly; supporting information is accurate and appropriate			

Paragraphs: Major ideas should be separated into paragraphs with appropriate indentation and formatting. An example of a major weakness in paragraphing is a full-length paper with no paragraph breaks.

Sentences: Examples of major errors include fragments and run-ons.

Usage: Examples of major errors include incorrect subject/verb agreement, tense, pronoun antecedent agreement, pronoun case and reference, and double negatives.

Mechanics: Examples of major errors include incorrect capitalization, end punctuation, and internal punctuation.

Additional Comments:

Adapted from material provided by N. Blue and B. Roane, Alamance-Burlington Schools, Burlington, NC.

Figure 6.2

Within each content area is the potential for relevance, extension, and impact on how adolescents view themselves, the world, and their place in it. Ultimately, these students will have to integrate the experiences of schooling into a personal philosophy of living and interacting. In the world of their future, the questions and problems that timelessly shape the content of the disciplines will be real, and adolescent learning will be tested. In this world, perspective, adaptability, flexible thinking, empathetic regard, personal commitment, and self-awareness will matter.

The Ongoing Question of Connection and Transfer

Transfer involves making a learning connection from one context to another. Mathematical skills, for example, are useful when a student is deciding how much tip to leave or calculating the savings on a pair of jeans. Learning how to organize an essay should carry over into the college classroom. The situations are similar, the path for connection is relatively straightforward, and transfer generally happens. A history teacher, however, might wonder why students do not see any parallel between the atrocities in Albania and Hitler's attempt to annihilate a Jewish population. The drama teacher might be surprised that students make no apparent link between the satirical content of a play and its historical context, and the language arts teacher might be surprised that students do not recognize the theme of "pride and prejudice" in their own relationships. For these more complex connections, the path is not so explicit, and it generally does not happen.

Perkins and Salomon (1989, 137) explained this prevailing problem accordingly: "We want students to make thoughtful interpretations of current events in light of their historical knowledge, but they have learned to remember and retrieve knowledge on cue. We can hardly expect transfer of a performance that has not been learned in the first place!"

Many teachers work hard to bridge the great "disconnect" between adolescent learning and its transfer value through the consideration of learning context. Successful teachers attempt to make the context for the new learning similar or familiar to where the transfer connections should be made. Sometimes, learning connections are not so apparently facilitated, and teachers have to work harder to help adolescents realize and use skills and knowledge from one context to another. Beyond a realistic context, teachers often have to "deliberately provoke" adolescents to think explicitly and metacognitively about where learning might connect, apply, or extend (Perkins and Salomon 1989). Figure 6.3 provides a few considerations concerning the ongoing challenge to teach for transfer.

The notion of transfer nevertheless remains complex (Bransford, et al. 1999). Learning is closely connected to the context in which it is learned, yet transfer is often contingent upon a good understanding of content. Conversely, since learning is contextualized, adolescents often have trouble adapting to a new situation if it varies from the original learning context. Problem-solving strategies are important to learn, yet adolescents need to be taught to reason through whether a strategy is appropriate or how it might be modified for use in a new situation. They need to be put in "what if" situations that expose them to a variation of a problem or context, thus teaching them to use skills or apply knowledge flexibly and strategically.

A critical player in the transfer process is, of course, the teacher (Fogarty 1995). They can ask questions that push for connections (Can you identify any situations in real life when people have freedom but act as if they live in Sameness?). They can prompt (Do you recall another time in history when immigration issues caused conflict in the United States?). They can model strategy and scaffold learning (Let's use a K/KN Board to give us a visual for our ideas about the problem or Let's think about the criteria for writing effective persuasion.). They can extend and generalize (Does the technique of the Surrealist painters remind you of any literary style? Can you see a use for this decision making grid in your own life?). They can alter a situation or a problem to encourage flexible and adaptive thinking (If we crumpled the pieces of paper, what impact might it have on the velocity? or Let's re-write Frost's poem in the style of e. e. cummings?)

Teachers can also structure interactive opportunities that enable adolescents to experience learning in a personal, motivational, and relevant way, such as simulation, role-play, seminar, debate, problem-based learning, and other realistic inquiry projects. Teaching for transfer is a complex, ongoing, and interactive process that must be intentionally orchestrated, guided, and mediated. Its goal is to help adolescents learn to use finesse and reasoning independently as they deal with a world shaped by unpredictable context. Ultimately, according to Perkins (1991), transfer is the true "measure" of teaching for understanding.

Learning for Life

The "brave new world" of the 21st century is one of international connection and unparalleled channels for rapid communication. Space, distance,

Teaching for Transfer

Don't Shortchange Content

- Select broad curricular concepts, principles, and themes that are "worthy" of transfer.
- Make connections across content areas.

A language arts teacher might organize literature around themes pertinent to adolescents' lives. For an exploration of human relationship, Bradbury's (1980) "All Summer in a Day," Frost's (1975) "The Mending Wall," and Lee's (1960) *To Kill A Mockingbird* could be used.

In physics, a student might be required to read a book by a science fiction author.

Consider Context

- Structure active, relevant learning experiences that promote understanding.
- Provide a wide, multiple range of comparable, analogous, and contrasting examples.

Through problem-based inquiry into historical events, adolescents can better understand social and political systems and hone useful research problem solving skills.

Civic action research projects can expose students to varying perspectives on pertinent societal issues and various ways civic action is defined.

Don't Leave Anything to Chance

- Be deliberate about coaching adolescents to generalize, apply, and adapt learning.
- Provide ongoing opportunity for reflection and assessment.

A social studies teacher can use questioning to help students critique Tiananmen Square documents and to connect this understanding to a real-world skill: What is important to consider in the critical analysis of sources? Do you think that what you read in the United States is always credible?

Students in an art class can critique their sketches in writing journals, and ultimately help to evaluate themselves through a portfolio and culminating exhibition.

Students who get into the habit of asking themselves, How can I improve on this presentation? How can I write a more logical paper or better contribute to discussion?

Figure 6.3

and time have been transcended, and, through technological advancement, the playing field is increasingly global. Powerful optical and holographic networking allow students to view Egyptian artifacts in Cairo, visit an art studio in Paris, and share ideas simultaneously with others across the world. Photons approximating the speed of light enable virtual communities and limitless exchange of information. In this new century, what people know, how they think, interact with and treat each other, how they view the world, what they choose to do with their ideas and creativity, and how they regard themselves are critical variables.

*Your
Ideas*

In his book, *Horace's Hope: What Works for the American High School*, Sizer eloquently expressed that the "dance of youth is timeless and beautiful in its awkwardness" (1996, 147). Adolescents desire to understand and to grow as human beings. This personal path is not an easy one, and they need guidance, encouragement, and the expectation to mindfully assess and thoughtfully reflect. The development of adolescents' creative spirits and positive attitudes carries long term implication for the culture and the broader society.

In his book, *The Abolition of Man: How Education Develops Man's Sense of Morality*, noted teacher, author, and theologian C. S. Lewis wrote that the "task of the modern educator is not to cut down jungles but to irrigate deserts" (1947, 24). He urged that teachers prepare young people to think for themselves and to consider the impact of personal actions and choices. This challenge speaks to the responsibility of teachers as they ready adolescents for the experiences ahead. Adolescents' education should be characterized by activity and purpose, relevance and challenge, and meaningfulness and responsibility. It should be filled with inquiry, questioning, exploration, interaction, and purposeful collaboration. Ideas should be shared, perspectives exchanged, examined, and developed, and opportunities given to delve deeply into important knowledge and carry it forward into their own lives.

The power to prepare adolescents well for an imaginable and unimaginable future rests with teachers in middle and high school classrooms across this nation and the world. The goal for adolescent learning is that they will be ready and inclined to continue the intellectual journey, or as Sizer wrote, the willingness to use their minds well "when no one is looking" (1997, 56). The quality of this preparation thus involves a deliberate effort to help adolescents realize the value of lifelong learning and the need for responsible, responsive living. Education should be more of a broadening, rather than a narrowing. It should be about gaining wisdom. Teachers who understand adolescents and their learning needs, who realize the challenge their future will bring, and who believe in their value and potential, agree.

ACTing
on the Adolescent-Centered Learning Principles Discussed in Chapter 6

Principle	*How I can put it into practice*
❑ Use content to help adolescents strengthen their thinking skills, develop personal competence, and acquire the strategies and dispositions for self–directed learning.	
❑ Explore the broad concepts and patterns of thinking that give each discipline its substance and distinction.	
❑ Realize the importance of instructional and curricular relevance.	
❑ Develop content around integrated themes, issues, and authentic problems and projects.	
❑ Plan for social interaction and collaboration.	
❑ Foster cognitive, interpersonal, and experiential connections.	
❑ Teach for transfer deliberately through authentic context, flexible adaptation, guided reflection, and purposeful extension.	

Internet Resources

The following Web sites for use by teachers and students were active at the time of printing.

American Library Association
Young Adult Library Services Association (YALSA)
> http://www.ala.org/yalsa

>> *Vision Statement*
>>> http://www.ala.org/yalsa/about/vision.html

American Psychological Association
> http://www.apa.org

American Schools Directory
Connecting Families & Schools
> http://www.asd.com/asd/asdhome.htm

The Apple Learning Interchange
> http://www.ali.apple.com

AskERIC
> http://askeric.org

>> *Virtual Library*
>>> http://askeric.org./Virtual

Association for Supervision and Curriculum Development
> http://www.ascd.org

Buffalo State College
> http://www.buffalostate.edu

>> *Index of /~beaverjf*
>>> http://www.buffalostate.edu/~beaverjf

>>> *Educational Applications of the Internet*
>>>> http://www.buffalostate.edu/~beaverjf/internet/index.htm

Center for Arts Education in New York City
> http://www.cae-nyc.org

Center for Disease Control and Prevention
http://www.cdc.gov
> ***National Center for Health Statistics***
> http://www.cdc.gov/nchs

Center for Mars Exploration Home Page
http://cmex-www.arc.nasa.gov

Classroom Connect
http://www.classroomconnect.com

Classroom Connect: IslandQuest
http://www.quest.classroom.com/island2000/splash.asp

Consumer Reports Online
http://www.consumerreports.org

Corporate Watch
http://www.corpwatch.org

CU-SeeMe Networks
http://www.cuseeme.org

Discovery Schools
http://discoveryschool.com
> ***Kathy Schrock's Guide for Educators***
> http://discoveryschool.com/schrockguide

EE Link –Environmental Education on the Internet
http://www.nceet.snre.umich.edu

Educational Web Adventures
http://www.eduweb
> ***Amazon Interactive***
> http://www.eduweb.com/amazon.html

Encarta Encyclopedia Online
http://encarta.msn.com/

Exploratorium
http://www.exploratorium.edu
> ***Institute for Inquiry***
> http://www.exploratorium.edu/IFI/index.html

Federal Consumer Information Center, Pueblo, CO
http://www.pueblo.gsa.gov

Federal Trade Commission
http://www.ftc.gov

Forest and Biodiversity Conservation News & Rainforest Information
http://forests.org
> ***Rainforest Information Center***
> http://forests.org/ric

Getty ArtsEdNet
http://www.artsednet.getty.edu

Global Schoolhouse at Lightspan
http://www.gsn.org/cu

International Society for Technology in Education
http://www.iste.org

Iowa Distance Learning Database
http://www3.iptv.org
> ***IPTV Interactive Media***
> http://www3.iptv.org/interactive
> > ***Earth Trail Mississippi River***
> > http://www3.iptv.org/interactive/miss

Jason Project
http://www.jasonproject.org/

Knowledge Integration Environment (KIE)
http://www.kie.berkeley.edu/KIE.html

Learner (Annenberg/Center for Public Broadcasting) – Journey North
http://www.learner.org/aboutacpb

Learning Through Collaborative Visualization (CoVis) Project
http://www.covis.nwu.edu

Math Forum
http://www.forum.swarthmore.edu

MATHCOUNTS
http://mathcounts.org

Microsoft Home Page
http://www.microsoft.com

NetMeeting
http://www.microsoft.com/netmeeting

Midstates Marketing
http://teacherzone.com

NASA Quest
www.quest.arc.nasa.gov

Interactive Projects
www.quest.arc.nasa.gov/interactive/index.html

National Council for the Social Studies (NCSS)
http://www.ncss.org

Standards and Position Statements
http://www.ncss.org/standards/teachers/standards.html

National Educational Computing Association
http://www.neccsite.org

National Geographic
http://www.nationalgeographic.com

National Geophysical Data Center
http://www.ngdc.noaa.gov

National Oceanic and Atmospheric Administration
http://www.noaa.gov

NCREL
http://www.ncrel.org

Ozline.Com—Tom March & Company
http://www.ozline.com

Webquests & More
http://www.ozline.com/webquests/

Webquests Rubric
http://www.ozline.com/webquests/rubric.html

School World Internet Education
www.schoolworld.asn.au

SchoolTech Exposition & Conference
www.schooltechexpo.com

Show-Me Center
http://www.showmecenter.missouri.edu

Skyrail Rainforest Cableway
http://www.skyrail.com.au

Skyrail – Tropeco
http://www.skyrail.com.au/tropeco.htm

Smithsonian Education
http://www.si.edu

Teaching Resources
http://si.edu/resources/resourcedir.html

Classroom Ready Lessons and Activities
http://si.edu/resources/lessons/lessons.html

Smithsonian Institution
http://www.si.edu

Center for Tropical Forest Science
http://www.ctfs.si.edu

Technology Education Lab
http://www.techedlab.com

K12 Educational Resources
http://www.techedlab.com/k12.html

Texas Computer Education Association (TCEA)
www.tcea.org

ThinkQuest 2000
http://www.thinkquest.org

ThinkQuest 2000
http://library.advanced.org

InvestSmart
http:/library.thinkquest.org/10326

Tiananmen: The Gate of Heavenly Peace
http://www.nmis.org/Gate/

U.S. Department for Education
www.ed.gov

Organizations of the U.S. Dept. of Education
www.ed.gov/offices

University of Michigan Education

http://www.umich.edu

Project-Based Science

http://www.umich.edu/~pbsgroup

Project Support Network
http://www.umich.edu/~pbsgroup/
psnet

University of Richmond Education

http://www.richmond.edu

Index of ~ed344

http://www.richmond.edu/~ed344

Index of Webquests
http://www.richmond.edu/~ed344/
webquests

Index of Papers
http://www.richmond.edu/~ed344/
webquests/paper/Paper1.htm

Wealth of the Rain Forest—Pharmacy to the World

www.rain-tree.com

Help with Rainforest School Reports

http://www.rain-tree.com/
schoolreports.htm

WebQuest Page

http://edweb.sdsu.edu/webquest/webquest.html

Web66 : AK12 World Wide Web Project

http://web66.coled.umn.edu

International School Web Site Registry

http://web66.coled.umn.edu/schools.html

Weekly World News Online

http://www.weeklyworldnews.com

World Bank Group

http://www.worldbank.org

Development Education Program: Education for Sustainable Development

http://www.worldbank.org/depweb

World Resources Institute

http://www.wri.org

References

Adams, D., and M. Hamm. 1999. Science: The truth is *not* out there. *Kappa Delta Pi Record* 35(4): 176–179.

Alexander, P. A., and P. K. Murphy. 1998. The research base for APA's learner-centered psychological principles. In M. M. Lambert and B. L. McCombs (eds.), *How students learn* (pp. 25–59). Washington, DC: American Psychological Association.

American Psychological Association Presidential Task Force on Psychology in Education. 1997. *Learner-centered psychological principles: A framework for school redesign and reform.* [Online]. http://www.apa.org/ed/lcp.html (accessed on 8/30/2000).

Ames, C. 1992. Achievement goals and the classroom motivational climate. In D. H. Schunk and J. L. Meece, eds., *Student perceptions in the classroom* (pp. 327–348). Hillsdale, NJ: Erlbaum.

Bandura, A. 1993. Perceived self-efficacy in cognitive development and functioning. *Educational Psychologist* 28: 117–148.

Barell, J. 1995. *Teaching for thoughtfulness: Classroom strategies to enhance intellectual development.* 2d ed. White Plains, NY: Longman.

Beamon, G. W. 1990. *Classroom climate and teacher questioning strategies: Relationship to student cognitive development.* Unpublished doctoral dissertation, University of North Carolina at Greensboro.

———. 1992–1993. Making classrooms "safe" for thinking: Influence of classroom climate and teaching questioning strategies on level of student cognitive development, *National Forum of Teacher Education Journal* 2(1): 4–14.

———.1993. Is your classroom "SAFE" for thinking?: Introducing and observation instrument to assess classroom climate and teacher questioning strategies. *Journal of Middle Level Research* 17(1): 4–14.

———. 1997. *Sparking the thinking of students, ages 10–14: Strategies for teachers.* Thousand Oaks, CA: Corwin Press.

———. 1999. Using assessment to your (and their) cognitive advantage. Paper presented at the annual meeting of the National Middle School Association, Orlando, Florida.

Begley, S. 2000. Mind explosion: Inside the teenage brain. *Newsweek* 19 (May): 68.

Bellanca, J., and R. Fogarty. 1991. *Blueprints for thinking in the cooperative classroom.* Palatine, IL: IRI/Skylight Training and Publishing.

Belton, L. 1996. What our teachers should know and be able to do: A student's view. *Educational Leadership* 54(1): 66–68.

Beyer, B. 1987. *Practical strategies for the teaching of thinking.* Boston: Allyn and Bacon.

Bloom, B. 1956. *Taxonomy of educational objectives (Handbook 1): Cognitive domain.* New York: McKay.

Bradbury, R. 1980. All summer in a day. In *The stories of Ray Bradbury* (pp. 532–536). New York: Alfred A. Knopf.

Bransford, J. D., A. L. Brown, and R. R. Cocking. 1999. *How people learn: Brain, mind, experience, and school.* Washington: National Academy Press.

Brooks, J. G., and M. G. Brooks. 1993. *In search of understanding: The case for constructivist classrooms.* Alexandria, VA: Association for Supervision and Curriculum Development.

Brown, A. L., and J. C. Campione. 1996. Psychological theory and the design of innovative learning environments: On procedures, principles, and systems. In *Innovations in learning: New environments for education* edited by L. Shauble and R. Glaser (pp. 289–325). Mahwah, NJ: Erlbaum.

Caine, R. N., and G. Caine. 1994. *Making connections: Teaching and the human brain.* (Rev. ed.). Menlo Park, CA: Addison-Wesley.

———. 1997. *Understanding the power of perceptual change: The potential of brain-based teaching.* Alexandria, VA: Association for Supervision and Curriculum Development.

Caine, R. N. 1999, April. *Best practices for brain-compatible classrooms.* Panel presentation at the 5th International Teaching for Intelligence Conference, San Francisco.

Center for Problem-Based Learning. 1996. *Professional development resource materials.* Aurora, IL: Illinois Mathematical and Science Academy.

Chaffee, J. 1997. *Thinking critically.* 6h ed.. Boston: Houghton Mifflin.

Codding, J. B., and R. Rothman. 1999. Just passing through: The life of an American high school. In *The new American high school* cditcd by D. D. Marsh, and J. D. Codding, (pp. 3–17). Thousand Oaks, CA: Corwin Press.

Cognition and Technology Group. 1990. Anchored instruction and its relationship to situated cognition. *Educational Researcher* 19(6): 2–10.

Cohen, J. (ed.). 1999. *Educating minds and hearts: Social emotional learning and the passage into adolescence.* Alexandria, VA: Association for Supervision and Curriculum Development and New York: Teachers College Press.

Collins, A., B. Beranek, and S. E. Newman. 1991. Cognitive apprenticeship and instructional technology. In *Educational values and cognitive instruction: Implications for reform* edited by B. F. Jones and L. Idol, (pp. 121–139). Hillsdale, NJ: Erlbaum.

Collins, A., J. S. Brown, and S. E. Newman. 1989. Cognitive apprenticeship: Teaching the crafts of reading, writing, and mathematics. In *Knowing, learning, and instruction: Essays in honor of Robert Glaser* edited by L. B. Resnick, (pp. 453–494). Hillsdale, NJ: Erlbaum.

Costa, A. L. 1991. *The school as a home for the mind.* Palatine, IL: IRI/Skylight Training and Publishing.

Covey, S. 1989. *The seven habits of highly effective people.* New York: Simon and Schuster.

Creating a climate for learning. September, 1996. *Educational Leadership* 54(1).

Daniels, H., and M. Bizar. 1998. *Methods that matter: Six structures for best practice classrooms.* York, ME: Stenhouse Publishers.

Danielson, C. 1996. *Enhancing professional practice: A framework for teaching.* Alexandria, VA: Association for Supervision and Curriculum Development.

Darling-Hammond, L. 1997. *The right to learn: A blueprint for creating schools that work.* San Francisco, CA: Jossey-Bass.

———. 1999, April. *The essence of powerful teaching.* Paper presented at the 5th International Teaching for Intelligence Conference, San Francisco.

Deci, E. L., and R. M. Ryan. 1998. Need satisfaction and the self-regulation of learning. *Learning and Individual Differences* 8(3): 165–184.

Dewey, J. 1933. *How we think.* Boston: D. C. Heath.

———. 1938. *Experience and education.* New York: Macmillan.

Diamond, M., and J. Hopson. 1998. *Magic trees of the mind: How to nurture your child's intelligence, creativity, and healthy emotions from birth through adolescence.* New York: Dutton.

Drier, H. S., K. M. Dawson, and J. Garofalo. 1999. Not your typical math class. *Educational Leadership* 56(5): 21–25.

Elkind, D. 1981. *Children and adolescents: Interpretive essays on Jean Piaget.* 3d ed. New York: Oxford University Press.

Eliot, T. S. 1976. The hollow men. *The complete poems and plays.* New York: Harcourt Brace and Company.

———. 1943. *Four quartets.* New York: Harcourt, Brace and World.

Ennis, R. H. 1987. A taxonomy of critical thinking dispositions and abilities. In *Teaching thinking skills: Theory and practice* edited by J. Baron and R. Sternberg (pp. 9–26). New York: W. H. Freeman.

Epstein, J. S. (ed.). 1998. Generation X, youth culture, and identity. In *Youth culture: Identity in a postmodern world* (pp. 1–23). Oxford, UK: Blackwell.

Evans, T. D. 1996. Encouragement: The key to reforming classrooms. *Educational Leadership* 54(1): 81–85.

Farley, R. P. 1999. A tale of two schools. *Educational Leadership* 56(5): 39–42.

Fatemi, E. 1999, September 23. Examples of digital content. *Technology Counts '99: Building the Digital Curriculum.* [Online]. Available: http://www.edweek.org/ sreports/tc99/articles/ summary~sl.htm.

Flavell, J. H. 1985. *Cognitive development.* 2d ed. Upper Saddle River, NJ: Prentice-Hall.

Fleming, D. 1996. Preamble to a more perfect classroom. *Educational Leadership* 54(1): 73–76.

Fogarty, R. 1995. Metacognition. In *Best practices for the learner-centered classroom* edited by R. Fogarty, (pp. 239–252). Arlington Heights, IL: IRI/Skylight Training and Publishing.

Fogarty, R., and J. Bellanca. 1995a. Capture the vision: Future world, future school. In *Best practices for the learner-centered classroom* edited by R. Fogarty, (pp. 55–72). Arlington Heights, IL: IRI/Skylight Training and Publishing.

———. 1995b. Cognition in practice. In *Best practices for the learner-centered classroom* edited by R. Fogarty, (pp. 73–100). Arlington Heights, IL: IRI/Skylight Training and Publishing.

———.1995c. What does the ultimate cooperative classroom look like? In *Best practices for the learner-centered classroom* edited by R. Fogarty, (pp. 183–203). Arlington Heights, IL: IRI/Skylight Training and Publishing.

Frieberg, H. J. 1996. From tourists to citizens in the classroom. *Educational Leadership* 54(1): 32–36.

Frost, R. 1975. The mending wall. In *The poetry of Robert Frost* edited by E. C. Lathem, (p. 33–34). New York: Henry Holt and Company.

Gallagher, J. J. 1997. Preparing the gifted students as independent learners. In *Connecting with the gifted community* edited by J. Leroux. Selected proceedings from the 12th World Conference of the World Council for Gifted and Talented Children, Inc.

Gallagher, J. J., and S. A. Gallagher. 1994. *Teaching the gifted child.* 4th ed. Boston: Allyn and Bacon.

Gallagher, S., W. Stepien, and D. Workman. 1995. School, science, and mathematics: Implementing problem-based learning in science classrooms. *School Science and Mathematics* 95(3): 136–146.

Gardner, H. 1983. *Frames of mind: The theory of multiple intelligences.* New York: Basic Books.

———. 1991. *The unschooled mind: How children think and how schools should teach.* New York: Basic Books.

———. 1993. *Multiple intelligences: The theory in practice.* New York: Basic Books.

———. 1999. *The disciplined mind: What all students should understand.* New York: Basic Books.

Geocaris, C. 1996–97. Increasing student engagement: A mystery solved. *Educational Leadership* 54(4): 72–75.

Gibbs, N. October 25, 1999. A week in the life of a high school. *Time* (pp. 67–82).

Golding, W. 1962. *Lord of the flies.* New York: Coward-McCann.

Goleman, D. 1995. *Emotional intelligence.* New York: Bantam Books.

Greeno, J. G. 1998. The situativity of knowing, learning, and research. *American Psychologist* 53(1): 5–26.

Hargreaves, A. 1997. Rethinking educational change: Going deeper and wider in the quest for success. In *Rethinking Educational Change with Heart and Mind* edited by A. Hargreaves, (pp. 1–26). Alexandria, VA: Association for Supervision and Curriculum Development.

Hine, T. 1999. *The rise and fall of the American teenager.* New York: Bard Books.

Jackson, S. 1996. The lottery. In *Point of view: An anthology of short stories* edited by J. Moffett & K. R. McElheny, (pp. 556–565). New York: New American Library.

Jensen, E. 1998. *Teaching with the brain in mind.* Alexandria, VA: Association for Supervision and Curriculum Development.

Johnson, D. W. 1979. *Educational psychology.* Englewood Cliffs, NJ: Prentice-Hall.

Johnson, D. W., and R. Johnson. 1983. The socialization and achievement crises: Are cooperative learning experiences the solution? In *Applied social psychology* annual 4 edited by L. Bickman, Beverly Hills, CA: Sage Publications.

Johnson, D. W., G. Maruyama, R. Johnson, D. Nelson, and L. Skön. 1981. Effects of cooperative, competitive, and individualistic goal structures on achievement: A meta-analysis. *Psychological Bulletin,* 89: 47–62.

Kagan, S. 1990. *Cooperative learning resources for teachers.* San Juan Capistrano, CA: Resources for Teachers.

Kantrowitz, B., and P. Wingert. 1999. How well do you know your kid? *Newsweek* May (pp. 36–40).

Kessler, R. 2000. The Soul of Education: Helping students find connection, compassion, and character at school. Alexandria, VA: ASCD.

Kohn, A. 1996. What to look for in a classroom. *Educational Leadership* 54(1): 54–55.

Lambert, N. M., and B. L. McCombs. 1998. Introduction: Learner-centered schools and classrooms as a direction for school reform. In *How students learn* edited by N. M. Lambert and B. L. McCombs, (pp. 1–22). Washington, DC: American Psychological Association.

Lee, H. 1960. *To kill a mockingbird.* New York: Warner.

Lewis, C. S. 1947. *The abolition of man: How education develops man's sense of morality.* New York: Macmillan.

Lightfoot, S. L. 1983. *The good high school.* New York: Basic Books.

Littky, D., and F. Allen. 1999. Whole-school personalization, one student at a time. *Educational Leadership* 57(1): 24–28.

Lowry, L. 1993. *The giver.* New York: Bantam Doubleday Dell Books for Young Readers.

Maeroff, G. I. 1982. *Don't blame the kids: The trouble with America's public schools.* New York: McGraw-Hill.

Marcus, S. A., and P. McDonald. 1990. *Tools for the cooperative classroom.* Palatine, IL: IRI/Skylight Training and Publishing.

Marsh, D. D. 1999. Introduction: An opportunity that comes once in a millennium. In *Preparing our schools for the 21st century* edited by D. D. Marsh, (pp. 1–9). Alexandria, VA: Association for Supervision and Curriculum Development.

Marzano, R. J. et al. 1992. *Dimensions of thinking.* Alexandria, VA: Association for Supervision and Curriculum Development.

Marzano, R. J., and J. S. Kendall. 1991. *A model continuum of authentic tasks and their assessment.* Aurora, CO: Mid-continent Regional Educational Laboratory.

McCombs, B. L. 1993. Learner-centered psychological principles for enhancing education: Applications for school settings. In *The challenge in mathematics and science education: Psychology's response* edited by L. A. Penner, G. M. Batsche, H. M. Knoff, and D. L. Nelson, (pp. 287–312). Washington, DC: American Psychological Association.

McCombs, B. L., and J. S. Whisler. 1997. *The learner centered classroom and school: Strategies for enhancing student motivation and achievement.* San Francisco, CA: Jossey-Bass.

McCullen, C. 1999. The electronic thread: Looking at technology learning labs. *Middle Ground* 3(1): 7–8.

Metivier, L. and L. Sheive. 1990. *A guide to STePS: Structured team problem-solving.* Baldwinsville, NY: STePS Associates.

Mid-continent Regional Educational Laboratory. 1999. Content knowledge: A compendium of standards and benchmarks for K–12 education. 2d ed. Aurora, CO: Author. [Online]. http://www.mcrel.org (accessed on 8/30/2000).

Miller, A. 1958. *Death of a salesman.* New York: Viking Press.

Nelson, G. D. 1999. Science literacy for all in the 21st century. *Educational Leadership* 57(2): 14–18.

O'Brien, D. G., D. R. Dillon, S. A. Wellinski, R. Springs, and D. Stith. 1997. Engaging "at-risk" high school students. *Perspectives in Reading Research* (12): 1–18.

Ormond, J. E. 1999. *Educational psychology: Developing learners.* 2d ed. Columbus, Ohio: Prentice-Hall, Inc.

Palincsar, A. S., and A. L. Brown. 1984. Reciprocal teaching of comprehension-fostering and comprehension-monitoring activities. *Cognition and Instruction* (1): 117–175.

Palmer, P. J. 1998. *The courage to teach: Exploring the inner landscape of a teacher's life.* San Francisco: Jossey-Bass Publishers.

———. 1998–99. Evoking the spirit in public education. *Educational Leadership* 56(4): 6–11.

Paris, S. G., and P. Winograd. 1990. How metacognition can promote academic learning and instruction. In *Dimensions of thinking and cognitive instruction* edited by B. F. Jones and L. Idol. Hillsdale, NJ: Erlbaum.

Paul, R. 1998. *Critical thinking: Basic theory and instructional structures.* Santa Rosa, CA: Foundation for Critical Thinking.

Paul. R., and A. J. A. Binker. 1995a. Critical thinking and the social studies. In *Critical Thinking: How to prepare students for a rapidly changing world* edited by J. Willsen and A. J. A. Binker, (pp.475–487). Santa Rosa, CA: Foundation for Critical Thinking.

———. 1995b. Socratic questioning. In *Critical Thinking: How to prepare students for a rapidly changing world* edited by J. Willsen and A. J. Binker, (pp.335–365). Santa Rosa, CA: Foundation for Critical Thinking.

Pea, R. D. 1993. Practices of distributed intelligence and designs in education. In *Distributed cognitions: Psychological and educational considerations* edited by G. Saloman, Cambridge, England: Cambridge University Press.

Perkins, D. N. 1986. *Knowledge as design.* Hillsdale, NJ: Lawrence Erlbaum Associates.

———. 1991. Educating for insight. *Educational Leadership* 29(2): 4–8.

———. 1992. *Smart minds: From training memories to educating minds.* New York: The Free Press.

———. 1999. The many faces of constructivism. *Educational Leadership* 57(3): 6–11.

Perkins, D. N., and G. Salomon. 1989. Teaching for transfer. In *Teaching thinking* edited by R. Brandt, (pp. 131–141). Alexandria, VA: Association for Supervision and Curriculum Development.

Piaget, J. 1928. *Judgment and reasoning in the child.* Translated by M. Warden, Trans. New York: Norton.

Pintrich, P. R., and B. Schrauben. 1992. Student motivational beliefs and their cognitive engagement in classroom academic tasks. In *Student perceptions in the classroom* D. H. Schunk and J. L. Meece (Eds.), (pp. 149–183). Hillsdale, NJ: Erlbaum

Public Agenda. 1999. *Kids these days '99: What America really think about the next generation.* New York: Author.

Raphael, J. 1996. New beginnings for new middle school students. *Educational Leadership* 54(1): 56–59.

Renzulli, J. S. 1998. A rising tide lifts all ships: Developing the gifts and talents of all children. *Phi Delta Kappan* 80(2).

Resnick, L. B. 1987. *Education and learning to think.* Washington, DC: National Academy Press.

———. 1991. Shared cognition: Thinking as social practice. In *Perspectives on socially shared cognition* edited by L. B. Resnick, J. M. Levine, and S. D. Teasley, (pp. 1–20). Washington, DC: American Psychological Association.

———. 1999a. Foreword to *The new American high school* edited by D. D. Marsh and J. D. Codding, (pp. vii–xi). Thousand Oaks, CA: Corwin Press.

———. 1999b (April). *Learning organizations for sustainable educational reform.* Paper presented at the 5th International Teaching for Intelligence Conference, San Francisco.

Roth, K. J. 1990. Developing meaningful conceptual understanding in science. In *Dimensions of thinking and cognitive instruction* edited by B. F. Jones, and L. Idol, (pp. 139–175), Hillsdale, NJ: Erlbaum.

Ryan, T. M. 1995. Psychological needs and the facilitation of integrative processes. *Journal of Personality* 63(3): 397–427.

Saloman, G., D. Perkins, and T. Globerson. 1991. Partners in cognition: Extending human intelligences with intelligent technologies. *Educational Researcher* 20(3): 2–9.

Sagor, R. 1996. Building resiliency in students. *Educational Leadership* 54(1): 38–43.

Schneider, B., and D. Stevenson. 1999. *The ambitious generation: America's teenagers, motivated but directionless.* New Haven: Yale University Press.

Schneider, E. 1996. Giving students a voice in the classroom. *Educational Leadership* 54(1): 22–26.

Schoen, H. L., J. T. Fey, C. R. Hirsch, and A. F. Coxford. 1999. Issues and options in the math wars. *Phi Delta Kappa* 80(6): 444–453.

Schoenfeld, A. H. 1985. *Mathematical problem solving.* San Diego: Academic Press.

Schunk, D. H. 1994. Self-regulation of self-efficacy and attributions in academic settings. In *Self-regulation of learning and performance: Issues and educational applications* edited by D. H. Schunk and B. J. Zimmerman, (pp. 75–99). Hillsdale, NJ: Erlbaum.

Schurr, S. L. 1989. *Dynamite in the classroom.* Columbus, OH: National Middle School Association.

Seibold, D. 1999 (April). The kids are all right. *Our Children,* 8–12.

Sharan, S, and Y. Sharon. 1976. *Small-group teaching.* Englewood Cliffs, NJ: Educational Technology Publications.

Shelton, C. M. 1999. How innersense builds common sense. *Educational Leadership* 57(1): 61–64.

Shuell, T. J. 1993. Toward an integrated theory of teaching and learning. *Educational Psychologist* 28(4): 291–311.

Simpkins, M. 1999. Designing great rubrics. *Technology and Learning* 20(1): 23–30.

Sizer, T. R. 1984. *Horace's compromise: The dilemma of the American high school.* Boston: Houghton Mifflin.

———. 1992. *Horace's school: Redesigning the American high school.* Boston: Houghton Mifflin Company.

———. 1996. *Horace's hope: What works for the American high school.* Boston: Houghton Mifflin Company.

Sizer, T. R., and N. F. Sizer. 1999. *The students are watching: Schools and the moral contract.* Boston: Beacon Press.

Slavin, R. E. 1980. *Using student team learning.* Baltimore, MD: Center for Social Organization of Schools, Johns Hopkins University.

Sprenger, M. 1999. *Learning and memory: The brain in action.* Alexandria, VA: Association for Supervision and Curriculum Development.

Stepien, W., and S. Gallagher. 1997. *Problem-based learning across the curriculum: An ASCD professional kit.* Alexandria, VA: Association for Supervision and Curriculum Development.

Sternberg, R. J. 1985. *Beyond IQ: A triarchic theory of human intelligence.* New York: Cambridge University Press.

Stiggins, R. J. 1994. *Student-centered classroom assessment.* New York: Macmillan College Publishing Company.

Strong, R., H. F Silver, and A. Robinson. 1995. What do students want (and what really motivates them)? *Educational Leadership* 53(1): 8–12.

Swartz, R. J., and D. N. Perkins. 1989. *Teaching thinking: Issues and approaches.* Pacific Grove, CA: Midwest Publications.

Sykes, W., and R. D. Reid. 1999. Virtual reality in schools: The ultimate educational technology. *Technological Horizons in Education Journal* 26(7): 61–63.

Sylwester, R. 1999. *A celebration of neurons: An educator's guide to the human brain.* Alexandria, VA: Association for Supervision and Curriculum Development.

Tapscott, D. 1999. Educating the net generation. *Educational Leadership* 56(5): 7–11.

Tell, C. 1999–2000. Generation what? Connecting with today's youth. *Educational Leadership* 57(4): 8–13.

The spirit of education. (1998–99). *Educational Leadership* 56 (4).

Tishman, S., D. N. Perkins, and E. S. Jay. 1995. *The thinking classroom: Learning and teaching in the culture of thinking.* Boston: Allyn and Bacon.

Tomlinson, C. A. 1999. *The differentiated classroom: Responding to the needs of all learners.* Alexandria, VA: Association for Supervision and Curriculum Development.

Torpe, L., and S. Sage. 1998. *Problems as possibilities: Problem-based learning for K–12 education.* Alexandria, VA: Association for Supervision and Curriculum Development.

Twain, M. 1954. *Adventures of Huckleberry Finn.* Garden City, New York: Junior Deluxe Editions.

U.S. Department of Education, National Center for Education Statistics. 1996. *The conditions of education, 1996.* Washington, DC: Government Printing Office.

Vygotsky, L. S. 1962. *Thought and language.* Cambridge, MA: MIT Press.

——.1978. *Mind in society: The development of higher psychological processes.* Cambridge, MA: Harvard University Press.

Vonnegut, K., Jr. 1968. Harrison Bergeron. In *Welcome to the monkey house: A collection of short stories* (pp. 7–13). New York: Delacorte.

Wiggins, G. P., and J. McTighe. 1998. *Understanding by design.* Alexandria, VA: Association for Supervision and Curriculum Development.

Wolfe, P. R. 1996. *Translating brain research into classroom practice.* Alexandria, VA: Association for Supervision and Curriculum Development.

Wolfe, P. R., and R. Brandt. 1998. What do we know from the brain research? *Educational Leadership* 56(3): 8–13.

Yoder, M. B. 1999 (April). The student WebQuest. International Society for Technology in Education. [Online]. http://www.iste.org/L&L/archive/vol26/no7/features/yoder/index.html (accessed on 8/30/2000).

Zimmerman, B. J. 1994. Dimensions of academic self-regulation: A conceptual framework for education. In *Self-regulation of learning and performance: Issues and educational applications.* Edited by D. H. Schunk and B. J. Zimmerman, Hillsdale, NJ: Lawrence Erlbaum Associates.

Index